Indira Gandhi

Letters to an American Friend

Dorothy Norman

INDIRA GANDHI

1917–1984

Indira Gandhi

Letters to an American Friend
1950–1984

Selected, with Commentary,
from Correspondence with
DOROTHY NORMAN

A HELEN AND KURT WOLFF BOOK

HARCOURT BRACE JOVANOVICH, PUBLISHERS

SAN DIEGO   NEW YORK   LONDON

Uncredited photographs are used through the courtesy of the offices of Prime Minister Jawaharlal Nehru and Prime Minister Indira Gandhi.

Library of Congress Cataloging-in-Publication Data

Gandhi, Indira, 1917–
  Indira Gandhi, letters to an American friend.

  1. Gandhi, Indira, 1917–   —Correspondence.
2. Norman, Dorothy, 1905–   —Correspondence.
3. Prime ministers—India—Correspondence.
I. Norman, Dorothy, 1905–   . II. Title.
DS481.G23A4   1984   954.04'092'2   85-13973
ISBN 0-15-144372-6

Designed by G.B.D. Smith

Printed in the United States of America

First edition

A   B   C   D   E

Contents

List of People   *vii*

Acknowledgments   *xi*

Introduction by Dorothy Norman   *xiii*

Part I
THE FIFTIES   *1*

Part II
THE SIXTIES   *65*

Part III
THE SEVENTIES AND EIGHTIES   *125*

Illustrations follow page 86.

v

People

Bhagat, Usha: Assistant to Indira Gandhi

Bunker, Ellsworth: United States Ambassador to India, 1956–1961

Crishna, Amie: Assistant to Indira Gandhi

Dhar, Rita: daughter of Vijaya Lakshmi and Ranjit Pandit

Fuller, Buckminster: inventor of dymaxion and geodesic forms; author of numerous volumes envisioning the transformation of society

Gandhi, Feroze: Indira Gandhi's husband; active in independence movement; editor and writer, *The National Herald;* member of Indian parliament

Gandhi, Mohandas K. (The Mahatma): leading Indian

spiritual figure; the "crest of the wave" of India's nonviolent struggle for independence

Gandhi, Rajiv and Sanjay: sons of Indira and Feroze Gandhi

Gandhi, Sonia: wife of Rajiv Gandhi

Hutheesing, Krishna: sister of Jawaharlal Nehru

Jayakar, Pupul: Chairman of Indian Handloom Board and Indian Arts Festivals; prolific author on Indian art

Lasker, Mary: leading U.S. philanthropist; president of Albert and Mary Lasker Foundation

Lord, Mary: United States representative to the United Nations Human Rights Commission; delegate to the United Nations

Mehta, Chandralekha (Lekha): daughter of Vijaya Lakshmi and Ranjit Pandit

Mountbatten, Edwina, Countess: wife of Lord Louis Mountbatten

Mountbatten, Louis: first Earl Mountbatten of Burma; last British viceroy of India

Naidu, Padmaja: Governor of Bombay State

Nehru, B. K. (Bijju): economist; Indian Ambassador to the United States; Governor of Assam; cousin of Indira Gandhi

Nehru, Fory: wife of B. K. Nehru

Nehru, Jawaharlal: father of Indira Gandhi; preeminent figure in the nonviolent movement for Indian freedom; first Prime Minister of India; world-renowned author

Pandit, Vijaya Lakshmi: sister of Jawaharlal Nehru; active in movement for Indian independence; Ambassador to the United States, the Soviet Union; High Commissioner to Great Britain; delegate to the United Nations

Roy, Sunil: Indian Consul General in New York

Sahgal, Nayantara (Tara): daughter of Vijaya Lakshmi and Ranjit Pandit

Tagore, Rabindranath: leading figure in Indian freedom movement; outstanding poet, author, composer, painter; winner of Nobel Prize for Literature, 1913; founder of Visva-Bharati University, Shantiniketan

Other people are identified in footnotes.

Acknowledgments

With gratitude for the gracious permission of Indira Gandhi to publish her letters; also to Pupul Jayakar for permitting me to include her correspondence.

With warm thanks to Ainslie Embree, Professor of History at Columbia University, for carefully checking the manuscript; to A. B. Patwardhan, Indian Consul General in New York, for providing data about various places and institutions; to Avis Klein for her excellent typing; to Ethel Bob and Elinor Weis for their valuable assistance.

Introduction

The primary aim of this volume is to share Indira Gandhi's letters to me; to illuminate and reveal the private individual behind the public image. It is in no sense a biography, or a political document.

These letters were not written for publication, and some material, not relevant to this volume, has been deleted. They are spontaneous expressions of friendship. Indira Gandhi and I wrote to one another over the years because it seemed natural to do so. I sensed her continued loneliness and her reaching out to speak with trust and without restraint.

Equally important to her, I learned, was the fact that my communications to her were sent only when the spirit moved me. I knew that her schedule was crowded; I did not expect her to reply to a specific note. It surprised me that the dependability of our relationship should so often buoy her; it amazed me, too, on how many levels we continued to be in touch.

Indira Gandhi and I met in October 1949. She had accompanied her father, Jawaharlal Nehru, India's first Prime Minister, on his initial visit to the United States. In the rush of glamorous events that took place in his honor, retiring, reserved Indira—just over thirty—remained largely in the background. I was touched by her modesty, dignity, quick intelligence. Intuition guided her; she was sensitive, elegant, unostentatious. Our eyes met in shared respect for certain persons or remarks—sometimes in amusement, at other moments in boredom with pretension. I liked her wry humor.

We sensed an immediate rapport: it was not necessary to ask questions or explain. Our preoccupations were similar: democratic freedoms, more advanced social welfare programs, eradication of poverty, nonviolence. Each of us was drawn to nature and beauty, to the same literature, art, dance, architecture, music. Both of us had experienced the ecstasy of having children, and the wonder of early-twentieth-century movements, with their passion for clarity yet subtlety, inventiveness, and renewal. We were equally in love with life-enhancing tradition. At moments of delight a radiance would transform Mrs. Gandhi's so often seemingly withdrawn, even sad, face.

Our friendship was based on mutual trust and convictions. Later disagreements did not mar it.

Prime Minister Nehru invited me to stay at his official Delhi residence in January 1950, for the celebration of India's birth as a republic. Having worked with American groups in support of the struggle for independence in the 1940s, I was delighted.

My room in the Nehru home was near the quarters of Indira, her husband, Feroze Gandhi, and their two young sons, Rajiv and Sanjay. Seeing the family on a daily basis intensified my already warm feeling for Nehru and Indira. As the Prime Minister's daughter, she carried out the role of hostess and confidante effectively, unobtrusively, and with grace; she assisted and worked well with her father in numerous other important capacities. Just as she had been nourished as a child by his letters written to her from prison, so now she absorbed much from him in the political and cultural spheres, although she was not herself drawn to power.

Her capabilities stemmed from an extraordinary willingness to work diligently and with concentration on detail and on what she considered good for India. Her resilience was astounding.

At the outset of my 1950 stay in New Delhi, Indira and I greeted one another with formal namastes, the palms-together gesture of greeting and farewell, and tentative smiles. Soon our New York openness and candor were reestablished. Nothing she said was off the record. We exchanged confidences and discussed events with relaxed spontaneity.

Because my sojourn in India was extended and so much was done for me—with such generosity of spirit— I found it difficult to know how I could give adequate, tangible evidence of my appreciation. It was simple to decide which gifts were suitable for Nehru and household members. What to present to Indira remained perplexing. She admitted at last, with restraint, that a few books and records would be welcome; after my protest that her request was too limited, she timidly confessed a wish for little suits for Rajiv and Sanjay.

We corresponded after my departure, with brief interludes and then a long one—from 1976 to 1980—for almost three decades.

There is little question that after she became prime minister in 1966 Mrs. Gandhi was often enigmatic and controversial. Nonetheless, she was, at root, dedicated to the democratic way of life for a free and united India. She was not cold, as often inferred, but warmly thoughtful and caring. An aristocrat of the spirit, she was as much at ease with international celebrities as with the most untutored peasants.

Her responses were invariably natural, effortless, artless. Wary of flattery, she was direct, in spite of an innate shyness; duly unimpressed by fame but moved by quality of achievement. She was British- and Indian-educated, and her interests were many, her travels wide-ranging. She was unspoiled and fearless, impatient with any suggestion that she was fragile. Determination and inner stamina served her well. She had blind spots, to be sure, as do we all.

Frequent family imprisonments before independence left in their wake a lifelong loneliness and hunger for love and friendship. The socialist leanings of her father greatly, but not entirely, affected Indira Gandhi's domestic policies. A reputation for even-handedness prompted world organizations furthering programs for social betterment to place her in positions of leadership. Like Nehru, she kept her nation nonaligned; she did not wish it to become Communist.

It is often difficult for the industrially, economically developed West to understand the tribulations of a people only recently liberated from colonialism. History and geography play their inevitable roles. At times a seemingly unbridgeable gulf appears to separate nations that should be at home with one another. Indira Gandhi said, "Home is wherever I go."

Part One

THE FIFTIES

Background of the Movement for Indian Independence, 1885–1947

The life of Indira Gandhi must be seen against the vast canvas backdrop on which is depicted the establishment of the Indian National Congress in 1885 and the surge of India's struggle for independence, initiated by those who protested against the British government's manifold forms of discriminatory measures.

Indira's grandfather Motilal Nehru became a leading Congress Party moderate in 1907. As early as 1912, her father, Jawaharlal Nehru, was a delegate to a Congress meeting. The moderates were not prepared to press for full independence, as was Mohandas K. Gandhi, who by 1919 was the dominant figure within the party. As the years went by, millions joined the freedom movement. It was Gandhi's nonviolent struggle for full independence that changed the course of modern Indian history.

In 1919–20 Motilal Nehru decided to dedicate himself totally to Gandhi; he gave up his highly successful legal practice and luxurious way of life. In becoming a Gandhian, he followed the example of his son Jawaharlal, who, having met and been overwhelmed by the Mahatma, had joined him in 1916. Fines, imprisonment, and other harassments were the painful lot of those who joined the Gandhian struggle.

Followers of Gandhi, unlike adherents of the Muslim League, were opposed to splitting India into two separate entities, yet on the very eve of independence, August 14, 1947, partition became a bitter fact and caused havoc in many ways. Pakistan was created as a separate state, in accordance with the wishes of the Muslim League. Eastern and western areas of the new country flanked the subcontinent of India. While hordes of Muslims and Hindus crossed borders for their self-protection, Gandhi sought to stem the violence between the two factions. To the distress of all, his pleas failed to avoid bloodshed.

Nehru had stated—also on the eve of independence—that he hoped India and Pakistan would cooperate and thereby establish close relations. On August 15, the problem became his, when he was sworn in as India's first prime minister.

The Retreat
Mashobra via Simla
October 13, 1950

Dorothy my dear,

My last letter must have crossed yours of the 7th September. I wrote it soon after the arrival of the elegant suits, for which many thanks again. The boys will be able to wear them now that winter is almost here.

In all your letters you mentioned the books and records that you have sent—these have not arrived nor is there any sign of them. But father says that things take about six months, so I am still hoping.

Gautam[1] gave a very vivid description of you, surrounded by masses of papers. What a job it must be sorting them out! Are you still at it, I wonder, or have you started writing. Or are you working on something else?

I carry on in Delhi until I feel that I am on the verge of collapse and then I dash off. This time, on top of everything, Sanjay (my youngest) had mumps and the woman who looks after the children is also ill, so I had just about enough. Specially as I was head of a committee for collecting funds for the Assam Earthquake relief.

I have brought the children up here—we are living in what is called The President's cottage but actually it is a huge house with ten or eleven bedrooms. Very English country house in style and simply impossible to keep warm. And it gets quite cold in the evenings. Much much colder than Delhi in winter. The garden is rather lovely. I am going down to Delhi on the 16th.

Your letter of the 5th has just come. It looks as if you have not received my letter—I wonder what happened to it. It is most annoying.

Anyway it is very sweet of you to write in spite of not hearing from me. Your letters are always welcome, although they give no news of you at all.

When you have a moment do write something about yourself.

As for me, I am full of ideas but I haven't the driving force and energy to execute them. One has to fight so much for every little thing. I was born bone lazy, so I have developed a system of dividing things into most important, important, less important and I fight only for the first, sometimes if I am very fit and energetic for the second as well.

What complicates life is our entanglement with other people. There is so much inter-dependence and so little understanding. And then growth. Every new experience brings its own maturity and a greater clarity of vision. Some people keep up to one, others get left behind—or else are able to share only a part of one's life. Do you think it is possible to have several sets of friends, each set moving in its own world and having no point of contact with the others? What else can you do if you are deeply interested in a large number of entirely different things and cannot find a single other person who shares all those interests? However, I do wish I were more interested in people as such. They amuse me and they irritate me and sometimes I find myself observing them as if I were not of the same species at all. Isn't that an awful thought?

It is late at night, the fire is out and my hand nearly frozen—so I shall close with my love.

Love,
Indira

1. Gautam Sahgal, husband of Nayantara Pandit, Indira's cousin.

Prime Minister's House
New Delhi
December 5, 1950

My dear Dorothy,

I am dashing off these few lines in a tremendous hurry—if I do not write when the thought strikes me, then the writing is put off indefinitely and usually never gets done at all.

You were so anxious that *All the King's Men*[1] should come to Delhi. Well, it has, finally. I went to see it a couple of days ago and I must say it is really good. Forceful and forthright and the acting superb, specially the supporting actress's. I wouldn't have missed it for anything.

But ever since I saw it I have been thinking of you and missing you. I like to see a good film with someone who would enjoy it in the same way but most people here seem to have missed the point of the whole thing, which irritates me intensely. It is silly to be irritated at such trifles, I keep telling myself—but all the same, not having anyone with similar tastes gives one a sense of loneliness and isolation which is not at all pleasant.

Much love to you,
Indira

1. Film based on Robert Penn Warren's novel.

The Residency
Bangalore
July 12, 1951

Dear Dorothy,

You are right. The longer one doesn't write, the more difficult it is to communicate.

I sent those few things—they are hand-blocked and printed old village designs from three quite different parts of India: the silk from Gujarat, the scarf from Kalimpong in the north-east, the handkerchiefs from Bengal—because I thought they would amuse you and also to tell you that you are very much in my thoughts. I haven't been able to write as I have been in a madder rush than usual, constantly travelling and have, besides, done something to my right arm which makes it a constant source of pain and irritation.

If someone asks me at the end of the week what I have been doing, I can't really answer but moment by moment the odd jobs seem important and urgent. On the whole it is a frustrating life. Long ago when I was a student in England, I went to Harold Laski[1] for advice about my studies. He said, "Young woman, if you want to amount to something you had better start on your own life right now—if you tag along with your father you won't be able to do anything else." But there doesn't seem to be any choice, in the sense that I *felt* my father's loneliness so intensely, and I felt also that whatever I amounted to, or whatever satisfaction I got from my own work, would not, from a wide perspective, be so useful as my "tagging" along, smoothing the corners and dealing with the many details, small but necessary, which in my absence he has to tackle himself with consequent loss of patience and temper! I'm not complaining. There has been the sharing of good things and bad. I am fortunate in having got just enough humour to tide me over the worst situations and enough love of nature to find beauty and delight in the most unexpected places. And there are so many other things—people and books, music and pictures and, above all else, my own children and the fascination of watching them grow and develop into two such very different persons.

However, now I must do something else as well. Write? But what about? I have such definite ideas about everything but they are all jumbled together. Perhaps writing would bring some kind of order and clear the path to future thought and work. The only thing (or is it an aspect of the same?) that I could do or feel readily attracted to, is some kind of literary or historical research.

What amazes me is the way I can write to you about myself—I haven't done this to anyone ever.

You have done such wonderful work for us on the Food Bill.[2] I don't quite know how to thank you. One says those two words so many times a day and so automatically that when one really means them from the heart, they somehow do not seem to be adequately expressive. And yet there are no other words.

We go to Delhi on the 17th and the next day I leave for Kashmir to join my children. We shall all be back in Delhi by the end of the month.

Love,
Indira

P.S. What an enchanting name Woods Hole[3] is!

1. British political scientist and economist.
2. In 1949, Prime Minister Jawaharlal Nehru and Indira Gandhi paid their first official visit to the United States, at the invitation of President Harry S. Truman. I was aware at the time of India's crucial need for food and economic assistance from America; it also was apparent that the nation, having been so recently liberated from colonial rule, was sensitive and reluctant to ask for aid. I knew, too, that the U.S. Congress could not act until it received specific requests from abroad for commodities or funds. Because, after I had been to India in 1950, I remained perturbed by her needs, I formed a broad-based Citizen's Committee to sponsor U.S. food aid for India.
3. Woods Hole, Massachusetts—location of the Norman summer home at the time.

From my reply:

Woods Hole, Mass.
August 1, 1951

Queer how space plays no role whatever when one feels concern. (Except that it can become a maddening barrier by way of separating—not by way of lessening caring.)

9

*You say now you must do something by way of utilizing
your creative or productive side. But you can't do that if you
merely continue to push down all the other sides. As for your
keeping everything under such perfect control: I think of that in
you so often. I am glad you feel free to talk to me, at least somewhat without reserve. How one longs always to be open and
honest. Only honesty and the feeling that one can be honest with
another can possibly satisfy. I have often thought how badly you
need to be loved and to be able to love to your full capacity. To
be honest and open about the most delicate things. There is so
much of the artist in you—in your search for form and line and
color, in the way you dress, and in your use of flowers—in every
way. And in the way in which you look at things.*

*Meanwhile—I am glad you like the name Woods Hole. And
I am glad you exist.*

Love,
Dorothy

Prime Minister's House
New Delhi
August 31, 1952

My dear Dorothy,

I'm just back from a very brief holiday in Kashmir with
my father. In Srinagar I bought a Tibetan bracelet for you
and decided to write to you on my return to Delhi. Imagine my surprise and delight to find your letter awaiting
me and its wonderful news [that you are coming to In-
dia]. It will be fun seeing you again after such ages.

I feel I am much more grown up now! With the weight
of the world on my shoulders! How long will you be
staying? I'm really excited about your coming.

Love,
Indira

In September 1952, the United States Department of State sent me to India to lecture on Indo-American cultural relations.

Meeting Indira Gandhi again in New Delhi made me realize how little I knew of her youth, despite our many talks. I had read that in her early years she participated in the destruction of her dolls and clothes made of foreign materials. She delivered impassioned speeches to family servants, in the great Nehru household known as Anand Bhavan. I was aware that Indira's mother had been ill, and imprisoned for her Congress Party involvement. Jawaharlal Nehru had described his career, including his frequent jail sentences, both in his autobiography, **Toward Freedom,** and in our conversations.

Clearly Indira did not have a normal childhood; indeed, she had none at all. Loneliness, difficulties, frustrations were her lot; yet I never heard her complain. I witnessed her love and care for her own two children, and how she spent the maximum possible time with them, despite manifold other duties.

I decided to question her about the years before 1950. She winced, but then smiled. "I hate to talk about myself."

"Then let's talk about Sanjay and Rajiv. Did their names have special significance for you and Feroze?"

"There is an 'a' at the end of Sanjay. Rajiv's full name is Rajivaratna: a combination of 'lotus,' for my mother's name, Kamala, and 'gem' for the first three syllables of 'Jawaharlal.' Rajiv was born when my father was in prison; he consulted everyone in jail about what we should call our first child."

Indira relaxed, so I inquired about her evolution:

"Did you suffer violence at the hands of the British? What significance did Gandhi have for you? Did politics play a great role in your early years?"

"Political activities invaded our home—first in Allahabad, where I was born—then throughout my youth. Not that I was attracted by them, but I was drawn in, beyond choice.

"Organized by Gandhiji,[1] the *khadi*[2] movement gained momentum when I was about nine. I can't remember much about my involvement, but the aim was to boycott English mill-made goods and to develop India's hand-loom weaving industry. Before his death Gandhi reminded me that I had served in the junior section of the movement.

"At about eight or nine I was taken to France; Jeanne d'Arc became a great heroine of mine. She was one of the first people I read about with enthusiasm.

"I was left to myself a good deal. My father and my mother, Kamala, were often in jail. My father didn't believe in giving directions about what I should do or feel. I had to decide things regardless of his or anyone else's ideas. That was both good and bad, but it helped make me independent. I learned from my parents by example; they made me aware that a certain standard must be maintained, even when nothing was said.

"Loneliness and having to act on my own may have made me mature more quickly than most other children. Few under ten are introduced into political circles or are permitted to hear adults' important political decisions."

"Did you suffer any violence as a child, because of your parents' role in the independence movement?"

"I was beaten up once when quite small. At thirteen I started a political movement of boys and girls in Allahabad. Our elders didn't like our being always underfoot. In a temper one day I said we should organize ourselves to help the Congress Party's fight for freedom.

We were called the 'Monkey Brigade,' serving as messengers, answering phone calls, sewing and hanging flags, doing all kinds of odd jobs for the grown-ups. Children couldn't picket against the use of foreign cloth, but we served water to those who had to stand out in the sun for long hours. We acted as a kind of junior spy system; it was rather effective.

"Membership in our group mounted into the thousands; children from every lane and street joined us. I spoke at a huge meeting but no one could hear me. There were neither loud-speakers nor funds, yet we did have a human loud-speaker—a man with a resounding voice. Someone would explain, 'We'll say something, then you bellow it out.' In a sense what we did was like an episode from the *Ramayana*.[3] The British jailed a number of Congress leaders; they soon were released, even though only temporarily.

"I went to school in Allahabad; then to boarding school in Poona, which was enjoyable. I remember most vividly the decision to make Gandhi's birthday a holiday. We did chores, things we thought might please him: working in slums or sweepers' colonies, helping with cleaning up and with games for children. On Tagore's birthday we learned his songs and sang them, instead of doing nothing.

"When Gandhiji fasted in behalf of untouchables, he hoped their condition would improve. But, as so often happens, others didn't follow through.

"At school we adopted a young girl—an untouchable; she received free education. A small child purposely was chosen, but she could remain only a short time. The question of her marriage came up and she had to leave. If untouchables' children could attend school and learn more skills, the sweepers' way of life could alter. I think, though, as my father does, that illiteracy has not made nearly the difference one would suppose. After all, plenty of literate people get nowhere, and vice versa. We need, of course, to wipe out illiteracy, but people of intelligence can do remarkable things under any circumstances, if given the opportunity.

"After Poona, I spent a year at the college founded by Rabindranath Tagore—Shantiniketan—near Calcutta. Then I accompanied my mother, who had fallen ill, to Europe. She died there in 1936.

"The following year I studied at Somerville, Oxford and took part in activities with my fellow students, many of whom wanted to know about India and Indian education. Their attitude was generally quite sympathetic.

"During the Chinese-Japanese War we made a collection for the Chinese. I helped not because of any positive anti-Japanese feeling, but because I believed war was wrong. World War II broke out in 1939.

"While in Germany in 1935, my mother and I had been very much aware of the Jewish problem. Few Jewish shops were open; no one dared enter them. One day I went into one with my father, who was with us at the time. The shop-keeper, dressed in black, fell on our necks. Although people behaved nicely to us, the atmosphere was tense. Many were rabidly Nazi. We knew, also, of course, about Mussolini's frightful actions.

"I was frequently ill for three years; in 1939 I spent the entire year in a sanitarium in Switzerland, but in the winter of 1940 I returned to England in the middle of the London Blitz. Because passage back to India was so difficult to book, I couldn't go home until the summer of 1941. I hadn't seen my father since he had been to the Sudetenland before the war. How terrified many there were also, but they were too paralyzed to say anything. In 1941 I reached India, but my father was in jail once again until autumn, when finally he was released."

"Didn't you have financial difficulties when your father was imprisoned, and you were in Europe during the war?"

"I never have thought about money very much, in part because while I was at the most impressionable age, my grandfather gave up his law practice. I have no memory of the luxurious way in which the family had lived, but we always were comfortable. I felt I shouldn't bother my elders about money, and I never have dreaded poverty and insecurity; I just don't think about the matter.

"I tried to reach England from Switzerland, but the war made it difficult to receive funds from home. In Lisbon, I needed money so I gave English lessons. If you feel you can earn something, the fear of being poor doesn't hang over you.

"On my return to India, I attended a number of student rallies and traveled with my father after his release from jail. In 1942, the Cripps Mission arrived from Britain promising dominion status in the future. That was unacceptable to the Congress Party.

"I worked with other women volunteers in Allahabad, but then the same year I married Feroze, who also was deeply involved in political activities. Almost immediately after our wedding, an important meeting was called to discuss the Cripps proposals.

"Feroze and I had taken a small, half-finished house, thinking we would complete it gradually. When decisions were being made just across the road, we set up an office in our own home; we moved in at once and lived in one room. Occupied with organizing women, I was out the entire day; Feroze was equally busy. By eleven at night, we would be too tired to have dinner; sometimes at two in the morning, we had something cold to eat.

"Finally we went to Kashmir for our honeymoon. Hearing that a Congress Working Committee had been formed, and that the 'Quit India' movement was evolving in Bombay, we quickly returned. Gandhiji wanted to ask the British to leave at once. Again the Congress leaders—my father and other major figures—were arrested. Feroze and I were tear-gassed.

"Back in Allahabad, Feroze went underground; I did 'coordinating' work: messages were quietly sent back and forth through me. One day I received advance information that my aunt Vijaya Lakshmi Pandit—my father's sister—and Lekha, her daughter, were to be arrested.

"Feroze thought we should hold a meeting; at it a virtual tug of war occurred. People were nearly torn to bits. Many were jailed, including myself. Everyone said the daughter of Nehru could not be arrested, but this was not so.

"I was imprisoned for eleven and a half months without a trial. A warrant was served against Feroze, who was jailed for eighteen months.

"At first, because of the spirit of the way in which we had courted imprisonment, discomfort didn't seem to bother us too much. Almost at once, though, I became ill; I ran a high temperature. Twenty of us, locked up together in barracks, were not allowed to receive news or letters from the outside. At times, if the matron happened to go to the movies, newspapers could be smuggled to us at 6:30 in the evening.

"I had begun to ask questions and to discuss things with my parents when I was seven. At ten I received my father's first letters to me from jail. Prison, of course, has played a decisive role in my life.

"The next lot I received—again from jail—are from 1933. My father had only one or two books with him, yet he wrote extensively about the history of the world. Since letters could not be sent, they were kept for me until his term was over.

"After my own release in 1943, I campaigned in the State Assembly elections of 1945. There was not much to do, but I could tell people to vote and why. Otherwise, before we moved to Delhi in 1947—the year we gained independence—I did little of a political nature, except to attend various conferences.

"When Britain transferred power in 1947, India and Pakistan were partitioned. I did nothing spectacular, but I did serve as a police-woman; I rushed out to stop fighting between Muslims and Hindus and succeeded in saving at least some lives. Such work was essential, but I didn't go about looking for trouble.

"I asked Gandhi whether he thought a police-woman was hidden within me. He replied, 'Work must be done. Go into the Muslim islands—into their isolated communities. Report what's happening.'

"I didn't know Delhi well. Gandhiji said, 'It's your business to learn about it.' At Town Hall, the rationing center, I found a young girl who did know Delhi. We, plus a few others, went about the city, reporting on curtailment of food rations, electricity and the water supply. Tensions were great. Since no one else would do it, we distributed grain ourselves. I always felt myself responsible for maintaining order and avoiding violence, for seeing that people's needs were met. Many Hindus and Muslims refused to go out because of fear.

"I arranged for a volunteer to accompany each sweeper as protection against possible violence. We organized so that from six in the morning until late at night— in spite of the curfew—workers could perform necessary chores. We received threatening letters for helping Muslims.

"Rumors spread that my father didn't understand the situation; that while we fostered good will for Muslims they were murdering Hindu children. Because our work was widely resented, a military guard was placed at our house; we had to travel by jeep, a gun protecting us.

"I was endlessly involved in getting medical help for those in need, in helping to achieve better food distribution and in doing what might be called 'peace work.' In various communities I asked Muslims which Hindus were 'good' and asked Hindus about Muslims. Then I held separate meetings of the 'good' from each group, ignoring bad elements. People said, 'We would like to work the way you suggest, but what will our neighbors think?' For a while persuading even a few to cooperate was difficult.

"We went into Muslim communities and, in spite of the danger of contracting cholera, drank from the cups offered us. To refuse would have been considered anti-Muslim.

"It took days to inspire trust. Finally we persuaded as many as twenty workers to help bring harmony between the opposing factions.

"Once widespread violence diminished, gradually we were able to go about normally. I found that if one wasn't afraid in crowds, nothing went wrong. I can't say I was brave. I simply went ahead; if some disagreeable incident occurred, I intervened. Somehow it would be over before I had time to think.

"One day, driving through a refugee camp, seeing about a hundred people chase a man, I asked the chauffeur to stop. I jumped out, ran into the crowd barefoot; no one knew who I was. I called out, 'You are not going to kill that man.' Someone yelled, 'We can kill him if we like.' I replied, 'You can, but I don't think you will.' They stopped and backed against the car. I took the man to a hospital.

"I worked in this manner until things were more settled; I felt utterly exhausted. After that I served on various hospital and refugee committees, but did no field work until this year's elections. I toured with my father a good deal, which was extremely strenuous; I always try to protect him at home or while traveling. I have found it helpful, if he couldn't show up at meetings, to talk in his place. I seldom had spoken to thousands, only to small gatherings.

"One afternoon my father was expected to address a group but he couldn't attend because of a previously scheduled event. I came in his stead, but arrived too late. Arrangements had been made for me to stay at the Government Residence, but I preferred to go to the home of the local candidate, his wife and daughter. That I should choose a simple place, instead of luxurious surroundings, made a deep impression. The opposition said it was not I who had come but someone pretending to be me. Others, however, insisted that if this were so, she would have selected the more elegant quarters."

"Was Gandhi's influence on your life strong?"

"I took many of my problems to him. I didn't invariably accept his views, but he always was present in my life; he played an enormous role in my development.

"One thing I specially noted was that he was merry; he laughed a good deal, whereas so many around him were grim. Nothing can convince me that people are at one with their work unless they're joyous about it. My father contends that unless you have a sense of humor, you are not a full human being.

"Gandhi didn't believe in painting pictures. He liked to look at them but objected to spending time to make things beautiful, whereas I think it essential to remove ugliness from the world.

"Gandhi's effect on Indian women has been crucial.

He helped them more than anyone. I am in no sense a feminist, but I believe in women being able to do everything. One can't forget that it was necessary to bring many out of purdah,[4] even at so late a date. Given an opportunity to develop, capable Indian women have come to the top at once.

"We are a poor country, so things should be as simple as possible, which doesn't mean they have to be ugly. Indeed, the simpler things are, usually the more beautiful.

"We should further develop our cottage industries and crafts; they shouldn't be commercialized. If they're to evolve in terms of contemporary life, they must change from within.

"Right now I am helping to arrange for the performance of tribal dances at our January 26 Republic Day celebration. Great numbers will be able to see ceremonials they couldn't otherwise witness, and villagers from remote areas will have an opportunity to meet others from different parts of the country. When I go to villages I love to join in tribal dances."

1. *Ji,* a suffix used as a mark of respect.
2. Indian hand-spun, handwoven cloth, the use of which was furthered by Gandhi and the Indian freedom movement to lessen dependence on foreign cloth.
3. The *Ramayana,* an ancient Hindu epic, attributed to the sage Valmiki. In it the two main forces, Rama and Ravana, represent, symbolically, light and darkness. To support Lord Vishnu, "The Ocean of Truth," celestial beings become incarnate as warriors in a monkey tribe; they oppose the forces of darkness.
4. Veiling and seclusion of women.

_____

While Indira Gandhi was speaking about painting, crafts, and tribal dances, I observed, as always, the beauty of her clothes; they were invariably unostentatious yet distinctive. On this day she was clad in a long, wide, printed cotton skirt. Over her blouse a short sari length was tucked in at the waist and thrown over her shoulder in traditional fashion. She remarked, with a smile, that she was eager to see such a style adopted, because of the greater freedom of movement it gave, and because of its practicality in hot weather.

I believed she had the inner, natural authority to influence life in India, not only in personal, but in far more significant ways.

Because I fell ill, my 1952 Indian trip came to an end after one month.

In 1953 I published part of this conversation as an interview in an Indian newspaper. I called it "India's Emerging First Lady."

I had mailed a typescript of our conversation to Indira before its publication. She gave me full permission to have it printed. But for reasons explained in the letter that follows, she requested that I put everything in the third person. Although I tried, the interview failed to come alive. After I explained this, she was satisfied with the interview as I had written it.

Prime Minister's House
New Delhi
September 9, 1953

Dear Dorothy,

I did know that you wanted to publish [the interview] and I have no objection to that. In my hurried reading—I got the impression that I was praising myself and that is what I don't like. If you could change that atmosphere it would be quite all right. As it stands it feels alien to me for I very rarely talk about myself and it is rather embarrassing to say that I did such & such. Perhaps if you could change the quotes and put it in your own language or some such thing.

This is written in great haste. You can imagine the rush of work and people after such a long absence. When I arrived in Delhi I was immediately entangled in the arrangements for Rita [Pandit]'s wedding—officially, I was in charge of decoration but so many other odd-jobs cropped up.

Love,
Indira

Prime Minister's House
New Delhi
October 12, 1953

Dorothy my dear,

You are quite incorrigible! I am blushing so hard after reading your article, I look like a cooked beetroot! It's a good thing we don't wear hats in India. I wouldn't be able to get into mine.

My latest venture is an appeal for funds for the buying of amenities for our troops in Korea. We—ten women—made the appeal the day before yesterday and already we have received over Rs. [rupees] 10,000. People have welcomed the move and seem particularly keen to send sweets for our festival of lights—Diwali—which falls on November 6th.

I think I have changed since we met. Or grown. Certainly I look older and I feel more positive somehow. This trip abroad—my first extensive travel alone—has done me an enormous amount of good. I put on some weight and had fun wherever I went. Even in the USSR. But the place

I liked best of all was Norway. I love its rugged beauty and the frankness and forthrightness of its people. The government seemed to me to be the most truly democratic and least encumbered with bureaucracy of all the countries I have visited. It may be, of course, that I was lucky enough to meet the right people and the right ministers!

Lekha and Tara came to dinner tonight. Lekha is quite distinguished. Tara is developing beautifully, and will I hope soon fulfill the promise which we glimpsed in her a few years ago.

How are you faring? Write and tell me of yourself when you have a moment.

Love,
Indira

Prime Minister's House
New Delhi
February 27, 1954

My dear Dorothy,

I know you are very busy, but I am writing this to ask a favor of you and if you cannot help me directly I hope you know of someone else who can do so.

It is sad that a large and growing city like Delhi, which attracts tourists from all over the country as well as from abroad, should be without a single decent theatre building. However, the matter has now been taken in hand by the Government—through the recently formed Academy of Drama, Dance and Music (Sangeet Natak Akadami). We are planning a national competition for designs for the building. We feel that while the exterior of the building should conform to the general architectural style of New

Delhi, at the same time the interior should incorporate all the latest innovations and fittings that are necessary to a first-class modern theatre.

I wonder if you could put me in touch with some person or firm in your country who could let us have detailed information on this subject? I should also be grateful for your own ideas.

Love,
Indira

My reply:

New York City
March 23, 1954

Dear Indira,

Lovely to hear from you. I am enclosing a batch of articles that may be of help to you.

The firm of Wallace Harrison (Rockefeller Center, N.Y.C.), helped greatly in the design of the UN building here. Mr. Harrison may be helpful to you. There also is a group of engineers at the Massachusetts Institute of Technology (Cambridge, Mass.) who have worked on acoustics, etc. If you get in touch with Professor Adams there, you may be able to procure advice on various problems. Professor Edward Cole at Yale University, New Haven, Conn., at the School of Drama there, has followed the development in theatres very closely. I believe that if you write to him, if there are any special questions you wish to take up with him, he may be of great help.

I imagine you have the usual regulations worked out with respect to the competition itself. I understand that the American Institute of Architects has worked out quite a good set of rules for competitions that tends to do away with most of the difficul-

ties into which one can run—(this for the protection of all involved).

Do let me know if there is anything further that I can do. Meanwhile, I send you warmest love,

Dorothy

Since I planned to see the hill towns of Italy during August of 1954 and attend the Jungian Eranos conference in Ascona, Switzerland, I suggested to Indira that she might care to join me. Erich Neumann, Mircea Eliade, D. T. Suzuki, Henry Corbin, Gershom Scholem, Paul Radin, Carl Kerényi and others of similar stature and interest would be there.

Mashobra
Simla Hills
July 4, 1954

My dear dear Dorothy,

It's always lovely to hear from you and the thought of going motoring in Italy is quite mouthwatering! I know and love Ascona too. But alas! I am so booked up through August that it is quite unthinkable to leave India. You can't imagine how sad it is for me because I really am longing to get out of the country for a while and talk and talk about everything under the sun.

I have not received any books or records from you recently—could you please post a list separately, so that I can check up.

I am in the midst of a domestic crisis, which would be quite a simple affair anywhere else in the world but here everything tends to assume enormous proportions. However, I myself am remarkably unaffected and considerably older, since you were here last.

I am truly sorry I cannot come but just your asking me has cheered me immensely.

Love,
Indira

Prime Minister's House
New Delhi
November 14, 1954

Dorothy,

Early tomorrow morning we leave for China. Today has been one of those days when I just couldn't sit and have not even had time for meals. With the result that I am practically passing out with hunger! Don't worry about me. I'm as tough as they come. If I weren't, I would have been dead long ago. But here I am—flourishing in spite of everything. I think it is because I can take pleasure from very little things. I am doing a tremendous amount of work these days but I haven't discovered my métier yet. And consequently am still looking for something in which I can put my whole heart and soul; to feel "that sense of utter exhaustion and peace that comes in dying to give something life."

Much love to you,
Indira

Prime Minister's House
New Delhi
May 31, 1955

Dorothy, my dear,

It is really unpardonable of me not to have replied to the very sweet letters you have been writing.

You have been much in my thoughts at various stages and I have often enough wanted to write but I cannot explain why it didn't come off! Sometimes of course there just wasn't the time.

What a life I have made for myself! Often I seem to be standing outside myself, watching and wondering if it's all worth the trouble. One acts the way one is made and it is only once in a lifetime that opportunity comes our way. I cannot say whether I have made good use of it or not.

It's certainly true that I have grown enormously since you saw me last. I am confident of myself but still humble enough to feel acutely embarrassed when all kinds of V.I.P.s come for advice and even help in their projects, as is increasingly happening. I still haven't gotten used to being on the Working Committee of the A.I.C.C.[1] (It is something like the National Executive of your political [parties].) Can you imagine me being an "elder statesman"?

My duties and responsibilities have also grown enormously. I have my finger in so many pies that it would take too long even to list them. And if you remember me and what a perfect tyrant of a conscience I have got, you will understand that this does *not* mean merely the lending of my name to some association or the attendance at committee meetings. It means hard work, planning, organizing, directing, scouting for new helpers, humouring the old and so on, in several fields—political, social welfare and cultural. Not to mention the visiting dignitaries—what a spate of them we have had this year!—and the constant entertaining and being entertained that it entails. The touring and public speaking. Besides all this, I have become almost a professional shoulder to lay upon for all those who are in trouble—the latest are two rather young widows whose husbands have died suddenly and very tragically. One of them (the husbands) was shot down by the Pakistanis in our latest "border incident." His widow is 26 and has three small daughters.

My first favourite—folk dancing—is merrily on its way and able to fend for itself. The current favourite—"community singing." As known in Europe and America this just does not exist in India, although we have folk songs that are sung by small groups, mostly women, at festival times. But this will soon be independent too. The "pet baby" is a recreation centre for 500 poor children. This is still at the plan stage and is going to shock a lot of people when it comes into being. I have "discovered" a young architect who has studied under Frank Lloyd Wright; even so it took a lot of doing to get him to plan something which is of no known shape or design and yet is practical and functional, with every room just where it is needed. We feel that it will be rather lovely when complete but most people do hate the new and unusual, so we are prepared for all kinds of criticism too.

As a trial, I have been running such a recreation centre on a small scale (70 children, all varieties, belonging to sweepers, M.P.s and government officials) in my own garden. A stupendous success. So much so that we have been forced to start a club for their fathers (not the officials!) and a welfare centre for the mothers! So you see the more one does, the more one can do and the more there is to be done.

I have been and am deeply unhappy in my domestic life. Now, the hurt and the unpleasantness don't seem to matter so much. I am sorry, though, to have missed the most wonderful thing in life, having a complete and perfect relationship with another human being: for only thus, I feel, can one's personality fully develop and blossom. However, and perhaps as compensation, I am more at peace with myself. One of our 17th-century poets has said "Go where thou wilt . . . if thy soul is a stranger to thee, this whole world is unhomely." I think I have come to a stage where home is wherever I go.

The boys are growing fast. They are in boarding school. I often go to see them at weekends and never cease to be surprised at the amount of ice cream they can consume at a sitting!

Love,
Indira

1. All-India Congress Committee.

Prime Minister's House
New Delhi
February 23, 1956

Dearest Dorothy,

I have postponed writing to you because I wanted to write a really long letter but there just does not seem to be any time for this.

I do not know why you should be baffled. I think you Americans make up your minds about something and then try to fit the facts in, instead of first trying to understand the facts and shaping the picture out of them.

We have not changed in any way except that as we go along we are gaining a little more confidence in ourselves. We are much more concerned with what is happening in our country, and with the many problems which are facing us. In fact our leaders are anxious to try and provoke even such problems as may not have arisen in the near future, realising that for the sake of India it is better for them to face these difficulties in their lifetime rather than risk any element of chaos afterwards.

Bulganin and Khrushchev[1] got a tremendous welcome here. There are many reasons for this but the main one was that they had accorded us a very wonderful welcome when we went to their country, and every Indian felt that we should repay their hospitality. At no time did anyone think that we were growing nearer to the communists, neither did Bulganin and Khrushchev think so. On the contrary my father availed himself of every opportunity to make our standpoint clear.

All those of us who have the opportunity of visiting the communist countries are very clear in our minds that we should not follow that path and we realise that we can only avoid this by strengthening our own organization and trying to prove to the people that ours is the better way.

It is because of this that I am taking a much more active part in politics. I have to do a great deal of touring in order to set up the Congress Party's Womens Section, and am on numerous important committees.

My main interest still remains as it was, much more in Art and Literature, but I feel that certain essential things have to be dealt with first.

How are you keeping—and what news of [your daughter] Nancy?

Love,
Indira

1. Nikolai A. Bulganin, Premier of the Soviet Union, and Nikita S. Khrushchev, First Secretary of the Communist Party of the U.S.S.R.

My reply:

New York
March 19, 1956

Dearest Indira,

I have your letter. Thank you for it. But how strange that you should have misunderstood the spirit of what I had written to you. The reason I said I was "baffled" was because I had seen certain things in print attributed to you that I could not believe were accurate quotations. I wrote that I was eager to correct wrong impressions. Your letter simply corroborated my feeling about you, and about your essential convictions. Yet, the very fact that I said that I wanted to do a piece to set things straight in connection with you should have made you know that I have implicit trust in you.

Isn't it strange that you should have come to precisely the opposite conclusion about what I meant, and even used such a phrase as "you Americans," to me of all people!

I continue to work for better understanding, and further support of what I believe in, in connection with India. I have just held meetings again for this purpose, as I have every year, in connection with attempting to build up public support for a more adequate and more understanding program of mutual cooperation with India. I do this, I can assure you, as much against a constantly negative spirit on the part of many Indians in this country, as against a negative spirit on the part of many Americans. I cannot tell you how difficult these last years have been with respect to doing things in an open spirit here in N.Y. I have written to you, and to your father from time to time, with the desire to communicate the anguish one feels about so much that is happening.

Much that has been built up by way of good will between Americans and Indians here has fallen away of late, and those of us who happen to be Americans, and who wish to continue to work in an outgoing spirit, have been having a hard time of it. I tell you this in all good faith.

I only hope it is true that you and your father are coming here. Is it so? I only hope that we can have a good talk, if you do come. And I will do anything I can for both of you while you are here, as you well know. Even including not having a good talk with you!

Do let me know if you are coming. And do let me know what I can do for you. I long to see you. I never lose my most personal, most affirmative feeling for you and for your father. This, you must know. Give him my warmest love.

Always devotedly,
Dorothy

Prime Minister's House
New Delhi
March 26, 1956

Dearest Dorothy,

Your letter of the 19th March has just arrived. I am so sorry I hurt you in my letter. I must confess I myself was not happy about what I wrote—for one thing I always seem to get very pompous when I am dictating!—and I had been meaning to write another letter all these days and had been thinking a great deal about you, but because of constant touring around the country there just was not a minute to sort out my thoughts. In the olden days I used to utilise plane trips for reading or writing work but now I get such a headache and am so much in need of sleep that that is all I can do.

I do understand all your difficulties and appreciate greatly the work that you are doing[1] and about which we hear from those returning from the States.

Here in India the situation is just as difficult. You must have read of Pakistan's increasingly belligerent attitude and the raids on our border areas. This has evoked such strong feelings all over the country that I doubt if people will listen even to my father on this issue. On my recent tour of Central India (I returned two days ago) everywhere I was asked why America was giving so much military aid to Pakistan.

I am accompanying my father to England and Europe but I do not think I am coming to the United States as I have not so far been invited, and I do not feel it would be proper for me to tag along unasked on a visit of this kind. Anyhow, as far as I know, my father is going to be there only for two or three days which will probably be spent in some quiet retreat with President Eisenhower, so there may not be an opportunity for him to meet others.

I wish I could come to the States. There is so much I want to discuss with you and other friends. I have thought many times about this but could not do so because it is so expensive and now as I am getting more and more involved in various fields of work it is becoming increasingly difficult to go out of the country for any length of time. Next year is our election year.

If I do go to the States and if it is at all possible to see you we must certainly find the time for having a good talk.

Is it not possible for you to come to England in the summer? We shall be there from June 22nd.

On these tours of mine at first I used to get physically exhausted, now I have got used to the physical strain but I still find it an emotional strain and I have a feeling of being drained out—as if I had given of my strength to people. The only thing that helps when I come back home is music and I have been listening to some of the lovely records you have sent me.

With love,
Indira

1. For U.S. food and economic aid for India.

Several passages in Indira's letters of 1956 reflect her confusion about a visit to the United States that President Dwight Eisenhower had intimated was to take place. At first, she was not included in the official invitation to Prime Minister Nehru; then dates were repeatedly shifted. Her pleasure was intense when plans were clarified, and she was to accompany her father.

Prime Minister's House
New Delhi
May 10, 1956

My dear Dorothy,

It is finally decided that I am coming to America and I have received a personal invitation from the President. I am thrilled, and am looking forward to meeting both you and Mrs. Lord! I do not think I know anybody else in New York. I suppose the Menuhins[1] will be in Europe.

I should love to stay with you in New York if that is quite convenient to you. I should like to leave my programme entirely in your and Mrs. Lord's hands as you have a fair idea of the sort of things I am interested in, and you are also the best judges of what I ought to see or do.

I do not think I need meet any Labour people on my

own. I should have liked to meet them if any such meeting has been arranged with my father.

About the programme you have drawn up, it seems a good one. I would love to see a play on the first evening—that is July the 7th. July the 8th is all right, keeping in view what I have said above about the Labour people, unless there is somebody special you would like me to meet. You can arrange the rest of the programme as you like. I hope you will keep plenty of time free for talks and if possible for shopping.

I hope I shall not have to make any speech at the U.N. lunch.

You could decide about coming to Washington later when we know my father's programme.

Please feel free to change any item or decide anything on your own. I think you know me almost better than I know myself.

With love,
Indira

1. Violinist Yehudi Menuhin and his wife.

Prime Minister's House
New Delhi
June 7, 1956

Dearest Dorothy,

I want to tell you that I would like to visit any projects for slum children or delinquent children if possible, but I am more interested in people who are active in different spheres. I should like to be present if my father meets trade union people or any other such group.

Yesterday, we had Mr. Walter Reuther[1] to lunch, and I must say I found him most stimulating. He gave us an entirely new picture of America, and one that we could appreciate and admire.

With love,
Indira

1. President of the United Automobile Workers of America.

Prime Minister's House
New Delhi
June 12, 1956

Dearest Dorothy,

I quite approve of all the changes you have had to make in the programme as there was obviously no way out. I am not terribly keen on visiting hospitals and housing projects unless there is something very special about them. So I thought it would be nicer to keep that time free for talks or for anything else that we might think of on the spur of the moment.

I am sorry about the theatre. It is one of the things we miss most in India. I hear there is a wonderful musical based on "Pygmalion." However, it will be so nice seeing you again that it does not really matter.

I am sorry you have had all this bother about the programme. I suggest now that you let things be just as they are and do not bother about changing anything.

As I am not now going out of New York on Sunday there will be no need for a police escort. Is this what you were going to check with the Mayor about? Please do not make any elaborate arrangements for me—they will only scare me!

Love,
Indira

Prime Minister's House
New Delhi
July 26, 1956

Dearest Dorothy,

It was a great disappointment to us both that the visit to the U.S.A. had to be put off. It was very sweet of you to invite me to come on my own but it would not have been possible for me to stay more than the four days originally allotted and I felt that it was hardly worthwhile to come for such a short visit.

I do feel strongly that I should come to the States, not only to present my point of view, but also to try and get to know your country. I am wondering whether it will be possible to arrange a visit after our elections are over. What do you think would be the best way to go about this? Is it better to come absolutely on one's own or to be sponsored by an organisation? There is heaps of time to plan and decide what would be really useful and worthwhile.

Yours,
Indira

———————

Prime Minister's House
New Delhi
August 25, 1956

My dear Dorothy,

I do not think it will be possible for me to come to America if my father decides to go this winter. I cannot leave India until the middle of March at the earliest.

With love,
Indira

Prime Minister's House
New Delhi
September 25, 1956

Dearest Dorothy,

Krishna has brought me the lovely records sent by
you. We returned to India [from England] only a few days
ago and have been immersed in piles of old newspapers,
correspondence and the various crises that always seem
to develop when one is out of town. I have not been able
to listen to the records yet but I am looking forward to
doing so—especially as the months to come are going to
be very strenuous ones.

As you know we are having our elections early next
year, and being a member of the Central Election Committee I shall have a great deal of work and responsibility. I not only have to go to most of the trouble spots in
different parts of the country, but have been given a whole
State—Assam—to look after. Needless to say all this is
besides one's normal work which is considerable.

I meant to write to you from London as I thought I
would have time when my father went to Ireland. I believe it is one of the loveliest countries in the world, and
I wish I had gone, but I felt that I should spend that time
looking at various aspects of Child Welfare work—especially that dealing with delinquent children. During the
Conference there was no opportunity of doing anything
except to keep changing one's clothes and keep dashing
from one official function to the next.

I am dashing this off in a hurry. If I do not send this
letter today it may have to wait months, as from tomorrow I start various meetings and tours.

With all good wishes, and much love,

Yours,
Indira

Prime Minister's House
New Delhi
November 24, 1956

My dear Dorothy,

I have been continuously out of Delhi on tour and since my return three days ago I have been immersed in rather important election meetings which have lasted the whole day through. On top of this we have a household of guests—U Nu[1] and others and I have "flu"! This is just to explain the delay in replying.

I do not know what to say to you as nobody seems to know what my father's programme is likely to be in New York. If we are to be in New York together I may have to be with him for some of his functions. I am sure you must be in touch with the State Department and Mrs. [Franklin D.] Roosevelt and you are the best person therefore to draw up my programme, according to the time that is free. I suppose all meals will be in common with my father. The rest I leave in your hands. If there is time I would like to pay a brief visit to the Museum of Modern Art.

Yours in haste,
Indira

1. Prime Minister of Burma.

Prime Minister's House
New Delhi
December 4, 1956

Dorothy dearest,

I am just dashing off these few lines in a hurry.

39

Everybody here seems most confused about the American programme.

This is absolutely the wrong time for me to be away from Delhi even for a day as we are in the midst of selecting our candidates for the next Election and I am greatly interested in this matter, so it is not at all possible for me to stay any longer than my father. In fact I may not even stop in London and come on here direct—thus saving a day. The programme, from what I have seen of it, seems to have the usual lunches and dinners and nothing else. I really do not know what to do about it. It seems rather a waste to spend all this money and go that long way for a couple of formal functions.

I have asked that I may be allowed to go to New York while my father is in Gettysburg, as this will give me one or two days quietly with you, but nothing has been decided yet.

As I have hinted before, there is a possibility of my not coming with my father. This depends on the results of one or two meetings which I am having in the next few days.

With love,
Yours in haste,
Indira

During the 1956 visit of Nehru and Indira Gandhi to the United States, a dinner at the White House, luncheons, and official talks, as well as interviews, took place in Washington. In New York they looked forward to moments of relaxation with individuals in the cultural sphere and to theatre, above all. I knew they wanted to see My Fair Lady, *by Lerner and Loewe, based on George Ber-*

nard Shaw's Pygmalion. *Unfortunately, they had time to go only to the last part of it.*

During that afternoon Indira and I saw Marguerite Duras's Hiroshima, Mon Amour. *The film by Alain Resnais struck both of us as magnificent.*

We then went directly to Mrs. Franklin D. Roosevelt's for tea. Later, Mrs. Roosevelt had a dinner, and after it a meeting of dignitaries, to honor Nehru, at the Carnegie Foundation.

In the morning, the practical, nonspendthrift Indira was elated by the simple kitchen gadgets in Macy's basement, and by its plastic dinnerware for her children. Lord & Taylor had a major display of India's tempting fabrics and crafts. The head of the store generously offered as a gift the few things Indira chose—a delightful gesture that was much appreciated. The bathing suits and negligées at Saks engendered delight. Indira was consistently modest in her purchases; her taste was invariably simple and classic. Visiting bookshops was tantalizing for her. She restrained herself, while yearning for practically every book she saw devoted to contemporary politics, literary criticism, sociology. She left the choice of records to me.

The schedule continued to be crowded. While Nehru attended official meetings, Indira and I visited the Museum of Modern Art and also the Metropolitan Museum, so she might see, among other work, Richard Lippold's sculpture Sun. *Mary Lord and I gave a luncheon at the United Nations in Indira's honor. I arranged for her to meet with heads of health and welfare groups, as well as to see several important welfare centers. We inspected both the interior and exterior of the magnificent, recently built Seagram Building.*

Blanchette and John D. Rockefeller III were deeply interested in India. They graciously invited Indira to their home in Tarrytown, which gave her her first opportunity to stay at a dignified, yet unostentatious American country home.

The Rockefellers were included in a dinner I gave for Indira before we went to West Side Story, *the stage version. The other guests were the distinguished French diplomat and 1960 Nobel Prize-winning poet Alexis Léger (Saint-John Perse) and his wife; Marian Willard, whose gallery showed distinctive American art, and her husband, Dan Johnson.*

For the next afternoon, Indira requested a gathering of progressive writers, editors, and artists, in whose ideas she felt she would be interested. In the evening we attended Samuel Beckett's Krapp's Last Tape *and Edward Albee's* Zoo Story.

———

Government House
Ottawa
December 22, 1956

Dorothy darling,

Just a line to say how wonderful it has been to be with you and to say thank you for all the trouble you took to make my stay just perfect. One has got into the habit of saying thank you for so many small things—the opening of a car door and other such normal attentions that when one really means something much deeper and more keenly felt, there just aren't the right words to say it in and one realizes the inadequacy of language.

Love and good wishes for 1957,
Indira

———

In January 1957, I spoke to Mary Lasker about the importance of Indira Gandhi knowing more of the United States. Too little time was left for travel during official visits. I had introduced the two women during Indira's Eisenhower visit; they liked one another at once. Mrs. Lasker generously offered to facilitate matters so that Indira might come to the United States on her own, unofficially. Unfortunately, it became impossible for this trip to take place, but Mrs. Lasker arranged Indira's program when she did visit California.

————

Prime Minister's House
New Delhi
January 10, 1957

Darling Dorothy,

On my return from Indore where I had gone for the Annual Session of the Congress Party I found letters from you had arrived. I am just dictating this brief note in haste as I may not be able to write a longer letter for some time.

Your news is indeed very exciting and I do hope that my trip [to the United States] will really materialise. However I cannot say "yes" or "no" just now until I have talked the matter over with my father. As you know he is very strict about our accepting presents and he may not approve of my accepting your friend's [Mary Lasker's] very generous offer. However I shall put the whole thing to him when he is in a good mood. Let us see what comes out of it.

It is very sweet of you to take up this matter so quickly and to take all this trouble. What fun if it does come through!

With lots of love,
Indira

P.S. I have had a talk with my father. He says I should go.

Love,
Indira

Prime Minister's House
New Delhi
January 31, 1957

Dorothy dearest,

Your letters. This is the most hurried scrawl. I hope you can decipher it! I have so much on my hands I don't know whether I'm coming or going! Early tomorrow I'm off on tour and do not even know the date of my return.

I don't mind where I stay in your house. I don't need an awful lot of room! I'd love to see something of the American Indians. Can all this be fitted in?

I don't know if I told you but on my return here I discovered why I was feeling so tired in the States. My blood was very anemic. I have been taking daily injections since then and am much better.

Love,
Indira

Prime Minister's House
New Delhi
May 25, 1957

Dear Dorothy,

I am not accompanying my father to Europe this summer as, because of the elections, my social welfare work was neglected, and I have now to catch up on this.

I have been thinking, and thinking about your plan, and trying to see if it can possibly work. I should love to come [to the United States] and it would be wonderful to see you and make other contacts and friends. There is so much to learn and so much to tell. However, apart from this personal aspect I do not know if such a visit is worthwhile in the present circumstances. There is a further complication; my father may be going to Japan in the autumn and is very keen that I should go with him.

It is becoming increasingly difficult for me to leave the country, firstly because of my own work, and secondly because it leaves my father so much alone. However, I am still thinking about this. It is difficult to plan until so many other things are decided—other people's plans, and so on.

Love,
Indira

Prime Minister's House
New Delhi
July 30, 1957

Dearest Dorothy,

Your brief letter of the 23rd of July has just come. I am hastening to reply as we are threatened with a postal strike and letters may not get out again in a hurry!

I am afraid the U.S. trip is off for the moment. It was only a dream! I am going to Japan for about a week with my father in the beginning of October. From then on we have a stream of foreign dignitaries—each year it seems to get worse. This year some of them are going to stay with us.

Apart from this the situation here is very complicated. We are in the midst of an economic crisis and it will not be possible to get any foreign exchange for travelling abroad. My father is so worried and has so much on his hands, apart from visitors, that I feel it would not be right for him to go off for any length of time.

In the economic drive it was proposed that we should move to a smaller house and this has raised many complications. Obviously we cannot move immediately and some changes will have to be made in this house for the interim period. These are some of the things which are tying me down to Delhi just now.

Do write and tell me what you are doing. I have been very depressed all this summer. It was a mistake not to go out as there is no place in India which does not have its problems so that it is quite impossible to have a real holiday in the country. Going out of the country even for a brief holiday is refreshing.

Much love,
Indira

P.S. What with the whirl of elections and all the work afterwards, I have been quite out of touch with people other than politicians—can you imagine anything more dreary?

Prime Minister's House
New Delhi
December 22, 1957

Dorothy dear,

A bad night and fits of giddiness have given me an excuse not to go to the office and I am snatching five minutes to write to you.

Ike's [Eisenhower's] trip [to India] was indeed wonderful. I knew it would be good but the actuality exceeded our expectations.

We have all read [Nevil Shute's] "On the Beach" and I can imagine it would make a good film.

I have my ups and downs but am as well as can be expected.

Love,
Indira

Prime Minister's House
New Delhi
April 17, 1958

Dearest Dorothy,

Thank you for all your letters. It is a comfort to hear from you and there is so much to tell. But the more one delays writing the more difficult it is to do so, for one just doesn't know where to begin.

I did write one short note acknowledging your letter but you don't seem to have received it.

This last year has been rather a gruesome one—busy of course but full of disaster, for our country.

I myself am feeling very unsettled—is it age, do you think? Ever since I was a small girl, there seemed to be some force driving me on—as if there were a debt to pay. But suddenly the debt seems to be paid—anyhow I get a tremendous urge to leave everything and retire to a far far place high in the mountains! Not caring if I ever did a stroke of work. Through the winter I felt carefree and light. Several people remarked that I looked "lit up from inside." As suddenly as it came that excellent mood has passed off. The heat may have had something to do with it.

It is 6 a.m. now but too hot to sleep. The temperature yesterday was around 104°F. A pall of dust is hanging over us, so that it is difficult to breathe.

The summer has come very early. Normally this sort of weather should come a month later.

I get up early these days to do a special set of exercises. It is a system (part of Yoga) that was taught us by an exceedingly good-looking Yogi. In fact, it was his looks, especially his magnificent body, which attracted everyone to his system, which is easy and practical. He is, however, exasperating to talk to—so full of superstition.

Thank you for your book [*The Heroic Encounter*[1]]—it is rather fascinating.

We have had two very interesting Americans—Charles Eames[2] and Buckminster Fuller. The latter was only passing through but managed to give me nearly five hours of higher mathematics. Quite exhausting but so stimulating.

After a long time yesterday I went to lunch with the B. K. Nehrus and had a quiet relaxed meal with Chopin's studies in the background. The lunch was for Tara and her husband who are breaking journey in Delhi on their way to Kashmir.

Mrs. Pandit arrived yesterday and will accompany Tara to Kashmir.

Our own summer plans are vague. I am looking forward immensely to Tibet but that will not be until much later.

Have you read a fascinating book—"The Third Eye"? Most absorbing, even when you discover later that the whole thing is a fraud—that the author is the son of an English plumber who has never been to Tibet!

This has become quite a pamphlet, so must stop now.

Much love,
Indira

1. By Dorothy Norman.
2. Outstanding industrial designer and innovative film-maker.

In 1958, Indira and I were invited to London to visit Mrs. V. L. Pandit, then India's High Commissioner to Great Britain. I had plans to attend various conferences on the Continent, as did Indira. We decided to meet first in London.

As guests of Mrs. Pandit, Indira and I attended The Duel of Angels *by Jean Giraudoux, in which Vivien Leigh starred.*

We then went to the Brussels Fair: diplomatic parties, a Congolese dance recital, Jerome Robbins's ballets, museums and the major national displays. We stood in the elaborate U.S. Pavilion. Indira said quietly, "They didn't have to do anything except have a fountain of clean water."

Prime Minister's House
New Delhi
May 17, 1958

Dorothy dearest,

Thank you so much for your letter—your understanding, and if I may put it that way, your moral support!

As usual this is a hasty scrawl. I am off to the hills with my father in a couple of days and am up to both ears in committees and other work which must be disposed of before I leave.

I have to be in India in August but I may have to go to Brussels for the Executive Committee and Conference of the International Council for Child Welfare. The dates are the 18th July to 27th July. It is still very much in the air. The finances, the time are both difficult, but they are promising. On our side too there is a feeling that the Asian nations are not adequately represented and therefore get bypassed at programme-making time. So I may go after all.

When are your conferences? Beginning or end of August? If the beginning, then perhaps you could come a little earlier and we could meet after all.

Delhi is hot as an oven and under a pall of heavy dust. As a compensation we have the most luscious fruit in this season and also the loveliest of flowering trees. The sky-line is splashed with vivid hues—red, orange, yellow, pink and many others.

Much love,
Indira

P.S. Wouldn't have time to go anywhere except Brussels—unless I go to London for a couple of days.

Delhi
June 4, 1958

Dorothy dearest,

Your letters.

I have not received any further news from the I.U.C.W. (International Union for Child Welfare), so that except for the date of the meetings, I am quite in the dark. It is not possible to judge how much and what time these will be. If we can manage the Exhibition at the Fair (which is huge but need we see every inch?) during the meeting days, we can go to London on the 21st evening. Otherwise we might stay on for a day or so. I am inquiring if it is possible to make a provisional booking on the 21st.

I am buying my ticket straight through to London so that does not present any problem.

Mrs. Pandit has sent me the London theatre guide but it is awfully difficult to choose from here. I should like to see a play with really good acting as that is something we miss so much in India. I don't think tickets to plays will be too difficult. Delhi is hell these days—hot as an oven with a pall of dust hanging over the city. One wishes one did not have to wear so many clothes. Bras are the worst because of the elastic and so on.

Love,
Indira

Prime Minister's House
New Delhi
June 7, 1958

Dorothy dearest,

A cable was sent off to you yesterday. There was some misunderstanding about dates. I find that my meeting starts on the 16th. So I shall leave Delhi on the 14th June reaching Brussels the next evening.

On the 16th, 17th I have the Executive Board of the International Union for Child Welfare. On the 18th and 19th is the meeting of the General Council. And for the 20th the World Child Welfare Conference. I shall attend the first two days, that is, the 20th and 21st and shall be free to leave Brussels on the evening of the 21st, providing of course that the Fair is not *too* tempting!

In Brussels I should probably stay with our Ambassador. I am not yet sure if they can have me.

In London I shall be with Mrs. Pandit. She is here just now but is leaving for Bombay en route to London on the 8th.

We are in the grip of a heat-wave. People are dying of heat stroke all over the place.

Love,
Indira

————

In Brussels, Indira and I again spoke of the possibility of her coming to the United States. As usual, this and similar plans were made and unmade, year after year.

————

Prime Minister's House
New Delhi
August 26, 1958

Dorothy darling,

It is such a bore not being able to express one's feelings. As you know I am quite exasperatingly inarticulate. So I cannot even begin to tell you what a joy it was to have you around and to talk to you. Somehow I can tell you things which I wouldn't dream of telling anyone. Each time I meet you, it helps me to sort myself out a little more.

The trip to Europe was exhilarating and I enjoyed every minute of it—again thanks largely to you. Even though we were not always together, I felt your presence and your support. Even though the return journey was tedious and tiring, I got off the plane fresh and exuberant.

People here don't like exuberance. Even at the airport I felt "different" and as if I did not fit in. People's glances were suspicious and just a shade disapproving.

What can one do but withdraw into oneself, in these circumstances? I really felt as if I had two wet blankets. Not only was this psychologically dampening but physically also, for I caught a bad cold!!

But seriously, I was in quite a turmoil and haven't got adjusted even now.

My various bosses feel that the world cannot revolve around its axis if I go out of the country in October, so the American trip is off once again. I think October will always be a difficult month. How is March or April for you?

I am glad you are having a stimulating time.

Love,
Indira

A Christmas card:

December 1958

This weird elephant brings all my love & feelings & good wishes for Christmas and the coming New Year.

Will we meet in 1959? And be able to give a more definite shape to something rather beautiful but so ethereal which began when we were together in Europe?

My thoughts are always with you and my love.

Indira

Prime Minister's House
New Delhi
December 20, 1958

Darling Dorothy,

The new President of Mexico [Adolfo Lopez Mateos]

has sent me an invitation to be a state guest—it hasn't yet been delivered but the news has been whispered in my ear by the Mexican Ambassador's wife.

Thank you for your letters, card and so on.

Love,
Indira

In 1959, the Albert and Mary Lasker Foundation, which gives annual Lasker Awards for outstanding contributions to science, invited me to attend and report on an International Planned Parenthood Conference in New Delhi.

Prime Minister's House
New Delhi
December 24, 1958

Dorothy dearest,

Your letter of the 16th has arrived just this minute and I am hastening to reply at once. Isn't this wonderful news! You will be most welcome.

I am afraid I may not be in Delhi for very long in February as I have to plan a number of tours.

Do let me know as soon as possible how long you are staying in India and whether you will be travelling around.

I had planned to visit Mexico and U.S.A. in April–May. I have some meetings at the end of March in Delhi.

I shall let you know as soon as my tour plan takes shape. I should like your advice about Mexico—how long do you think I should stay there and in Peru? Will it be better to go to Mexico first—in April and then come to the U.S.A.?

Love,
Indira

Prime Minister's House
New Delhi
December 29, 1958

Dearest Dorothy,

How lovely to hear your voice out of nowhere! And how wonderful that you are coming over to India.

I don't think you heard what I was saying. Will you be back in the states in the beginning or end of April?

Do advise me how to divide up my time. Should I go to Mexico first? How long should I spend there? Much as I want to, I don't think it will be possible to include Peru— will it?

I have not been at all well for the last month or so. And have a simply dreadful cold and cough.

May 1959 bring you joy.

Love,
Indira

During this same period, plans for Indira's trips to Mexico and South America—like those to the United States—were constantly changed. I conferred with United States Ambassador to India Ellsworth Bunker about a possible unofficial Indira visit to America. Her proposed journey to Mexico became entangled with the one we planned for the United States. To complicate matters further, she was invited to come to New York on Air India's inaugural flight to the United States.

Prime Minister's House
New Delhi
January 3, 1959

Dorothy dearest,

Your letter of the 24th December arrived a few days ago and we immediately made inquiries.[1] The information you have asked for will be ready to collect, I cannot send it to you immediately. I propose to make a copy of the relevant extracts from your letter and to send them to the Ministry of Health.

This will not involve my spending any time. As it is I have a rather heavy tour programme scheduled for February and March and cannot have more than brief glimpses of you in between—depending upon how long, and exactly when, you are in Delhi.

It may be difficult for me to accompany you back as your journey will be a long and halting one. You must have received my last letter. I am awaiting your reply before giving a definite answer to the Mexican Embassy. In it I had asked for your suggestions for the trip and whether it would be better for me to go to Mexico first and then come to the U.S.A. Much as I would like to I do not think I could fit in other countries.

If you would let me know your definite dates of your stay in Delhi we can even fix up some appointments in advance.

Love,
Indira

1. About the medical reports relating to Planned Parenthood requested from the Indian Ministry of Health.

July 21, 1959

My dear Dorothy,

I wish telepathy were more advanced and I could convey my thoughts to you without having to write a letter.

A veritable sea of trouble is engulfing me. On the domestic front, Feroze has always resented my very existence, but since I have become President [of the Congress Party] he exudes such hostility that it seems to poison the air. Unfortunately he and his friends are friendly with some of our ministers and an impossible situation is being created.

The Kerala situation is worsening. This movement is not petering out as the Communists claim but gathering momentum. The women, whom I have been trying to organize for years, had always refused to come into politics. Now they are out in the field. Over 8000 have been arrested. I have heard that in Europe and perhaps in America my father is being blamed for not taking any action. He has given a very good lead from the beginning but he is incapable of dictatorship or roughshodding over the views of his senior colleagues. More and more I find that he is almost the only one who thinks in terms of ideology rather than personality. I cannot write much in a letter but you would be surprised that some of the ministers whom we had considered the most anti-Communist are now supporting the Communist government of Kerala. My father cannot go against the wishes of the Home Minister, for instance. It is a very ticklish situation.

I don't know if any of this will make sense to you, since you are not aware of the details of the background.

Most American newsmen suffer from such Nehru-phobia that they are unable to gauge the situation and are therefore indirectly helping the Communists, since any weakening of the Congress organization can only advance the cause of Communism in India.

It has been a dreadfully hot summer.

Thank you for all your letters. I have not had the time to read the other papers you have sent.

Love,
Indira

During my 1959 trip to India I saw much of Indira when the conference meetings had terminated. She was more caught up in Indian politics than I had ever seen her before. She had just been elected Congress Party President. Rumors spread that Nehru had made this possible. He told me he had had nothing to do with it; Indira confirmed this. I went with her to villages, where she spoke. She received a warm reaction, although she was not yet accustomed to addressing large crowds. Her ability to do so increased noticeably in the days ahead. Her sincerity and resistance to playing up to audiences inspired trust.

After the Planned Parenthood Conference in India, I continued my trip throughout South and Southeast Asia. Thus it was some time before I could be in contact with Indira again. She sent a number of messages, which I received only on my return to New York.

Dorothy darling,

If you believe in telepathy, you will know that I have been thinking a great deal of you these last months. Many a time I wanted to write but I was so depressed that I felt I would be bound to convey some of it in my letters!

Apart from the mental depression there was a physical one too. I lost a lot of weight and have been quite shaky on my feet, fainting off a couple of times and so on. However, I'm better now. I'd better be as I'm off at the crack of dawn to Calcutta on my way to Bangkok.

I'm really writing to thank you for the wonderful records—all through this dark period, the only thing that seemed to help was music and poetry. Some of my loveliest ones are from you.

Do you know Dylan Thomas' *Under Milk Wood?* An English friend sent it to me some time ago but I only got time to listen to it recently. Isn't it simply wonderful?

Pupul was here this afternoon. She's a stimulating person. I feel I know myself better after a talk with her. Are most people not just a split personality but several personalities? I feel I am and I have learnt to make all the separate personalities quite friendly with each other. But I still don't know how to present them to the world. Different people see different mes!

Pupul said she would write to you to ask for a list of the poetry or drama records that are now available in the U.S.

Much love to you.

Indira

Prime Minister's House
New Delhi
October 10, 1959

Dorothy dearest,

I am feeling utterly ashamed of myself for all your letters and for the bras you sent through Pupul. I kept postponing writing to you as I thought I would write a long letter myself but as the possibility of this still seems remote I thought I would send these few dictated lines just to let you know I have been receiving your letters and your gift.

The bras literally saved my life as I did not have any just then. Because of the climate the elastic gives way—that is why they have a short life.

I have been getting into a bigger and faster rush and this month's programme is really quite an impossible one. What makes it worse is that I am far from well. The doctors have discovered a stone in the kidney and I have a great deal of pain most of the time. If I can hold out that long I propose having the operation next February in London. However, you know what happens to most of my proposals!

Thank you for Lillian Smith's book [*One Hour*]. It arrived a short while ago just when I was searching for a novel to take on tour. I leave for Bombay and Maharashtra in a couple of hours.

Much love,
Indira

Prime Minister's House
New Delhi
October 21, 1959

Dorothy dear,

Your letter of the 15th has just arrived and I am dictating this reply as otherwise I may never write.

I came back from tour a couple of days ago and leave again even before the crack of dawn tomorrow for five days, then again a couple of days or so in Delhi and then to the U.P. [United Provinces]. Such is the programme right up to the end of November.

The tour in the Maharashtrian part of Bombay state has been most hectic—one thousand miles by car and 150 largely attended meetings, all in five days!

I am afraid I am not looking at all radiant just now. Thanks to the dust I had lost my voice completely and am even now croaking because of a bad chest cold.

The operation is for a stone in the kidney. Normally there would not have been any hurry but being jolted up and down on bad roads is the worst possible thing. However, I do not see how I can possibly have it before February. The tour programme will take me on to the end of November, if not part of December as well. In January we have our Congress session, so February is the earliest I can manage. I had a vague hope of being able to go to London for this but my personal plans so seldom come through that I hesitate to make any.

I have also been invited to Singapore to speak to a Ladies' Association and am tempted to go next year.

Love,
Indira

Dorothy dearest,

You are a gem. I am always overwhelmed by friendship—perhaps because there is so little of it. Your letter was so sweet and generous.

There was so much talk of the "stone"—my kidney stone—that we decided to give it a name. Padmaja Naidu [Governor of Bombay] is in Delhi for the Governor's Conference. She is inclined towards grandiose names and supplied "Jewel in the Lotus"! (Indira is one of the names of the lotus.) As a compromise we have settled on Jule. Jule has been on his best behavior and I have not had an attack of pain for sometime. The doctors had felt that my constant touring—especially on bumpy roads—might be harmful and that Jule may damage the kidney. So now I am going in for an old Indian system of medicine, which assures the strengthening of the kidney tissues. Even two or three treatments have made a difference in my urine report.

However, the long range prospect for the operation remains. I am unable to decide the date or place. My father would rather I had the operation in India, so that he could be around. But February is beginning to be hot and therefore not good for healing of wounds.

At the moment I feel that I should go to Europe in February or March regardless of the operation. It would be lovely if you were there too. But don't bank on my plans—you know how unreliable they are.

In the meantime, Mrs. Bunker has told me that there is some new treatment in the States—that such operations may become out of date because the stone can be split by some super-sonic treatment! I have asked her to find out more about this. It sounds quite exciting.

All sections in India, with the solitary exception of the

Communists, feel that I have done a good job [as Congress Party President] and there is tremendous pressure on me to continue for another term. It has been tough work—sometimes exhausting, but always a worthwhile experience. I have gained tremendously in self-confidence. But I do not wish to continue for many reasons. The routine part of the work takes too much time and is too confining. I have felt like a bird in a too-small cage. Also I feel that I have now established myself and will be able to do quite a lot even from outside, besides being free to take up any particular project—there are some which are urgent.

I did not know when I would get the chance of writing, so just as we were leaving I yelled to Mrs. Crishna, my secretary, to write to you. She will have told you that the *I Ching* book arrived only a couple of days ago and we have not yet received the book of poems you mention.

With love,
Indira

Part Two

THE SIXTIES

Indira's desire to explore new territory persisted, in spite of the painful reality of an operation she had to have in the late fifties. The inaugural flight of Air India to New York materialized, and other proposed journeys continued to be under consideration.

———

Prime Minister's House
New Delhi
February 12, 1960

Dorothy dear,

Just a very hurried line to say thank you for your letters.

My operation will take place on the 17th of February here in Delhi at the Willingdon Nursing Home. The surgeon is from Bombay—Dr. Shantilal Mehta. Pupul knows him and says he is good.

I hope my future programme will be decided before I go into hospital on the 16th. If I cannot write myself I shall get someone to let you know.

The print by Morris Graves[1] has just turned up— Pupul brought it when she came to see me the other day. It is beautiful. She is getting it framed for me.

We have just had an alfresco lunch for Khrushchev starting off, by special request of his grand-daughter, with a snake-charmer's performance. Unfortunately the snake refused to cooperate.

Love,
Indira

1. I had given Indira *The Time of Change,* a silkscreen print by American artist Morris Graves.

Prime Minister's House
New Delhi
April 11, 1960

Dorothy dearest,

I hope your lost twenty pounds have not wandered across the ocean to me. I have put on weight, not much but too much, if you know what I mean. Thank you so much for all your letters and thoughts. I am utterly ashamed of myself for not writing earlier. My thoughts have been with you but I have been feeling so lazy that the very thought of lifting a pen was exhausting! My father was keen that I should go to London with him but I did not feel that it would be worthwhile in this state of mind. So I am staying back. I may go to the hills, perhaps Darjeeling.

I may just stay on in Delhi and be roasted! The new Mexican Ambassador is asking to see me. If he renews the invitation, shall I offer to go there in September? I should then stop off in the U.S. on my way back or first, whichever is the best time. In the meantime I am not doing anything and not wanting to do anything. It is not a satisfactory feeling. I <u>must</u> find the right vocation.

Love,
Indira

Raj Bhavan
Bombay
May 2, 1960

Dorothy dearest,

The surgeon who operated upon me resides in Bombay, so I came down here with my father. (He was on his way to the U.K.) I have been involved with X-rays and the like and have been given a clean bill of health! So there is no need for a medical check-up in N.Y.

It has finally been decided that I *do* go on the inaugural flight [of Air India to the United States], arriving New York on the 14th and leaving again on the 20th. I should like to do whatever you think would be the best and most convenient to *you*. I'd love to stay with you if you'd like that. Or I could stay a couple of days at the Hotel.

It is difficult to plan out a programme from this distance. I should like to meet the [John D.] Rockefellers if they are in town. I should like to do some shows. I am not yet back in harness and everybody feels that before I

do immerse myself in anything I should be quite frivo-
lous. So please decide.

While I am there we might as well try to make some
rough plan for Mexico in September or October.

When I leave New York, I am joining my father in
Istanbul. We return to India via Beirut. Is there anything
I can bring?

Love,
Indira

Prime Minister's House
New Delhi
June 16, 1960

Dorothy dear,

Your letter of the 23rd June reached me just as we
were leaving Srinagar (Kashmir) where we had a most
delightful quiet three week holiday. I read it in the plane
and my mind was full of ideas and thoughts to be con-
veyed to you. But as soon as we landed in Delhi I got so
involved with matters pertaining to the threatened general strike by Central Government Employees that there
wasn't a free moment.

The strike succeeded partially in Bombay and Calcutta and in a couple of small towns. Delhi remained
practically normal. However we had a critical situation in
Assam with riots between Bengalese and Assamese. I am
going there with my father tomorrow.

I wonder if you have received a letter which I wrote
from the plane after leaving New York.[1] I also sent you a
post card from Lebanon or Syria, I forget which.

Right now New York seems so far away—was I really
there or was it just a hallucination?

I do want to talk too—the holiday in Kashmir, my first real holiday in I don't know how long, is partly responsible.

Must stop now.

Indira

1. For the return trip after Air India's inaugural flight to New York.

Prime Minister's House
New Delhi
June 27, 1960

Dorothy dear,

I had lunch with the Bunkers yesterday and we went over your suggestions, point by point. The Bunkers will be writing to you. It is more or less definite that I arrive in the States the first week of November. The date of return is still undecided. I would like to be back by the 14th. November 14th is my father's birthday and a very heavy day for him.

The Bunkers asked if I should like to be away a fortnight. What do you think? Does it interfere in any way with the sort of programme you had in view?

I have got elected to the Deputy-Presidentship of the International Union for Child Welfare—so I shall have to at least go and visit their office in New York. About the Asia House reception or meeting—I am not quite clear what is going to happen then or whether I shall be able to make a worthwhile contribution.[1]

Love,
Indira

1. A large dinner at the Asia Society was planned to honor Indira, at which she was to speak.

Dearest Dorothy,

I have just been for a brief visit with the Bunkers and I am dashing off this letter in great haste as I am leaving Delhi tomorrow at 5 a.m. In my last letter I gave a hint that I would have to change the date of my stay in the U.S. because of a plan to send me to Africa. A tentative itinerary has now been drawn up.

I shall leave Delhi on the 21st September and go for a day or two each to Kenya, Northern Rhodesia, Nigeria, Ghana and Mali. The African tour ends at Dakar on the 6th October. From here on, I think, there are two alternatives.

Either I go to New York via Madrid or Lisbon (I am not sure of the plane services). This would probably bring me to New York around the 9th October. I can stay there until the 1st November. Mr. Bunker suggests that I then go to New Orleans, Sante Fé or any other place in the Southern States of the U.S. reaching New York on the 6th and staying in the U.S. until the middle of the month.

If at all possible, I should like to cut down the duration of the South American tour to ten or twelve days, but this would bring me to the U.S. that many days earlier.

Mr. Bunker prefers the second alternative as he feels that it will be interesting for me to be there on the election day and, perhaps, to meet the new President.

These dates may be more suitable for all political people. Or, will they be completely exhausted after the excitement and hard work of the election campaign? On the other hand, except for Mrs. Roosevelt's Buffet Supper, there does not seem to be anything in your programme which would conflict with the elections. These dates are still not final but they do give a rough indication and I should be glad if you could let me know which alternative would suit you better.

I have not yet spoken with the Mexican Ambassador and much depends on his views too. Originally, we had told him that I would reach Mexico around the 9th October. If he insists on that date, then the whole programme will have to be recast and I shall have to begin my tour with Mexico.

I have not discussed the details of the U.S. programme with the Bunkers as we were all rather in a hurry today. I hope to discuss it when I go to lunch with them on the 25th.

Love,
Indira

Prime Minister's House
New Delhi
August 2, 1960

Dorothy dear,

It is very very late—practically the 3rd August and I can hardly keep my eyes open as I got up at 5 this morning!

What with the Naga[1] and other preoccupations, External Affairs have been too busy to deal with my programme and so nothing seems to be definite except that I *am* going.

I have not replied to anybody not even to the Bunkers regarding my being a guest of the U.S. Government.[2]

I was hoping to have your advice about it—will it mean a lot of stuffy entertaining?

Everything should really get finalized within this week.

Love,
Indira

1. The Nagas, in Nagaland State, in northeast India, had resorted to violence, apparently in an attempt to achieve secession.
2. Ambassador Bunker had obtained a U.S. government grant, which entailed no obligations of any kind. Indira would be able to travel where and as she wished.

Prime Minister's House
New Delhi
August 23, 1960

Dorothy dear,

Dr. [Sarvapelli] Radhakrishnan, our Vice-President, wants me to be part of our delegation to UNESCO. The meeting is from the 14th November to 10th December but he says I need not stay the whole month. He also wants to put me on the Executive Board. I think it might be a worthwhile thing to do, don't you? But it does cut into the U.S. visit.

I have not heard from the Bunkers, so yesterday I wrote to them. I have no idea about the programme. Anyhow, you and the Bunkers are much better judges than I am about such matters, so I shall leave the planning in your sizeable hands.

I leave India on the 18th September for Kenya, Uganda, Tanganyika—then a day in Rome on the 28th (address of Embassy of India) and on to Nigeria, Ghana,

Guinea and Mali, flying from Dakar to Rio on the 8th October. Then Buenos Aires, Montevideo, Santiago, Lima, Caracas, Havana, Mexico City on the 25th and up till the 6th November. Arriving New York same day 6th November at 17.45.

The books have finally arrived two days ago. Thank you so much. I don't know which to read first but have already dabbled in several.

Love,
Indira

Prime Minister's House
New Delhi
August 29, 1960

Dorothy dear,

Your letter written on the plane came just as I was going to a meeting of our Children's Museum Committee. I learnt that Dr. Grace Morley[1] has arrived but has gone to Calcutta this morning. Pupul will try and meet Dr. Morley if she returns before Pupul leaves for Bombay.

Pupul must have spoken to you about a young person, Dr. P. Sahasrabudhe whom she would like to have as Director in over-all charge of the museum and adjoining children's recreation-cum-education centre (Bal Bhavan). Dr. Sahasrabudhe is at present connected with the New York University and is with [Victor] D'Amico of the Museum of Modern Art.

I have asked the Ministry of Education to send him the relevant papers as well as the blueprints of the plans for the children's museum so that we need not waste time on preliminaries.

I am glad to hear that Bijju and Fory will be in New York as I am not now going to Washington.

We are having an industrial fair in the winter months of next year in New Delhi. It would be wonderful if the children's carnival could be sent out for it. I hope Mr. Bunker can do something.

I wonder whether we can get any help from the Natural History and Science and Industry Museums in Chicago for our Children's Museum.

The last two days we have been having meetings of our Indian Council for Child Welfare. The Council has made some progress for this last year and has done some satisfactory work at different levels—international, national and in the States. The two big handicaps that remain are lack of finance, lack of trained personnel and most important of all the reluctance of the Government to state any definite policy regarding child welfare. I was wondering, with all the numerous foundations abounding in your country, whether it would be possible to get some funds for this child welfare work in India. This could be either for definite projects or more generally for our Council's work.

Love,
Indira

P.S. I am so sorry to hear of your mother's illness. I do hope it was not severe and that she is already on her way to recovery.

I should have loved to stay with you but the general feeling here is that since Mrs. Crishna is accompanying me, it would perhaps be better if we both stayed at a hotel.

I am off to Allahabad in a short while, then after two days in Delhi I go South for a Women's Convention.

1. Head of National Museum in New Delhi.

The death in 1960 of Indira's husband, Feroze Gan-
dhi, had represented a heartbreaking blow to her. Despite
their early closeness, they had drifted apart. Yet it was still
Feroze she loved, just as she cherished their children.

She had rushed to the hospital when he was taken ill,
and it was of the greatest comfort to her that she learned
from him, shortly before his death, that he had always truly
loved her, and no one else.

Prime Minister's House
New Delhi
September 21, 1960

Dorothy—

I am still quite weak with shock and although the burden of sorrow seems heavy enough even now, I feel it can only increase as the numbness wears off and one is faced with reality. I first met Feroze when I was thirteen and he eighteen—he had saved a fistful of sticky sweets for me! He proposed three years later when I was 16. And since then we quarrelled over every conceivable subject, but the strong bond of affection never weakened. We grew together and whatever each of us achieved, it was for and with the support of the other. When my mother died and at all times of stress and difficulty, he was by my side even if he had to travel across continents to get there. I feel as if I were all alone in the midst of an unending sandy waste. And still life has to go on.

I had wanted to cancel the whole trip but it is with the greatest of difficulty that my father and others have agreed that the Africa part may be given up. I shall probably cut out South America too and start the trip with

Mexico. That means that the U.S. schedule remains the same. I may be able to arrive a couple of days earlier.

Thank you for your call.

Indira

P.S. Although Feroze had been proposing to me since I was 16, it was on the steps of the [Basilica of] Sacré-Coeur that we finally and definitely decided. It was the end of Summer, Paris was bathed in soft sunshine and her heart truly seemed to be young and gay, not only because we ourselves were young and in love but because the whole city was swarming with people who were young at heart and in a holiday mood. 1937 was one of those years when the awareness of the war to come was still veiled. One changes all the time, so perhaps I do more often now but up till now I had somebody to whom I could pour out my thoughts—even if there was a lack of attention and sympathy—and with the removal of that outlet I have to look outward.

Prime Minister's House
New Delhi
September 24, 1960

Dorothy,

Just a few moments ago I told Amie Crishna that I did not feel like writing letters! But there's one thing I must tell you—we met about three months ago but I'm not the same person now. Neither to look at nor deep down inside. Maybe by the time I reach N.Y. I should feel better—less empty—but I don't think I can ever again be quite the same. Isn't it strange that when you feel full, you are also light as air but when you feel empty and hollow you feel an enormous weight crushing you down? Will I ever be free from this burden or be able to touch and see without feeling "the heartbreak in the heart of things"?

Indira

Merida, Yucatan
Mexico
October 31, 1960

Dorothy dear,

Thank you for your letters and the programme. The second letter enclosing the programme reached me first! We have lost two days out of our already brief stay in Mexico. The first due to bad weather—we had to hang around the airport waiting for the plane and now we are stuck here because of a strike by the ground crew at the airports! The strike may go on forever but we are trying to get picked up by a special plane of Prince Albert of Belgium.

Mexico is so similar to parts of India and yet utterly utterly different.

About the other thing [Feroze]—I'd like to talk but it is so difficult. Right now that hollow empty feeling seems to leave me—the grief or rather the missing him is a veil surrounding me & covering me from all sides. I feel as if my luck has run out and have no confidence in myself. Also the sixth sense or "seeing eye" (as somebody called it) is quite shut off.

Love,
Indira

P.S. The Belgians have sent word that their plane is overloaded because of their purchases! They are only ten in a plane with twenty-one seats! So the government is sending a special plane. What a life.

The long-dreamed-of private visit to the United States took place late in 1960. Indira's wish to see something of American Indians was to be fulfilled.

She arrived in Dallas from Mexico; I met her there. We saw the city and, in particular, the Frank Lloyd Wright Theatre. We went to Arizona and then to New Mexico, where we stayed in Santa Fé. The writer Mabel Dodge Luhan (who was married to a Pueblo Indian) invited us to lunch at her gracious home in Taos. The lovely and expansive British painter Dorothy Brett was present. She told Indira she longed to come to India and ride on a large elephant, under a huge umbrella. Much laughter. She and Indira liked each other at once.

Brett took us to the Taos Pueblo, where she knew various Indians. We drove around the magic area. Alexander Girard, the splendid American designer, and his wife invited us for dinner at their home which was filled with folk art from all over the world.

After we were alone, Indira spoke of Feroze's death. Tears flowed. She had really loved him always, with her virginal first enchantment. She had depended on his love for her, beyond all the vicissitudes that had beset and seemingly separated them. "He really loved me, after all," she said, with a youthful wistfulness that revealed a touching vulnerability behind the disciplined "public mask."

In New York we went to bookstores, concerts, record shops, theatre. At Yale University, Indira was awarded the Howland Memorial Prize for outstanding achievement.

80

As a result of Pupul Jayakar's interest, I also took In-
dira to the Museum of Modern Art, so that she could see
its Children's Carnival. Victor D'Amico had created it to
provide stimuli for young people who visited the museum.
He stressed the tactile, sensory, and visual qualities of the
materials on view, encouraging the children to paint what
they experienced, in terms of their own imaginations. In-
dira was enthusiastic about D'Amico's project and thought
it would be relevant to Indian children. Interest was aroused,
and funds raised in New York, to transport the Carnival
to India, under the guardianship of D'Amico and Sahas-
rabudhe. The two showed it with enormous success in In-
dia. Many new materials were discovered that further
contributed to the sensibility of the young people who at-
tended it. The project was installed at the Children's Mu-
seum, Bal Bhavan, in New Delhi, under the guidance of
Sahasrabudhe.

In the latter part of 1960 my mother was periodically ill.
While Indira was in New York, I had news of her that
worried me. I rushed to Philadelphia, and remained with
her until she died in December.

———

Embassy of India
Paris
November 19, 1960

Dearest Dorothy,

Your face, as you went down in the lift, has been
haunting me all these days. How are you, my dear? I have
purposely not written earlier as I had a feeling I should
not burden you with letters just now. You were already
so burdened with anxiety.

What news is there of your mother? You should not
have hesitated a moment to rush to Philadelphia. We all

understood perfectly and there were a number of persons to see to my departure which was on time and according to schedule.

Paris is deadly dull—at least this conference is. The thought of having to live through four whole years of this is most depressing. We are imprisoned in these vast halls from 9 or 10 a.m. right up to 7 or later, including Saturdays. In between, lunch is with some delegation or another and the evening is full of receptions until quite late. I am now told that I shall not be able to leave until around the 13th December. In between I may go to West Germany for a couple of days.

You have done so much for me, not only this time but over the last years, that I hardly know where to begin to thank you. I enjoyed my stay in the States and I think for the first time really began to understand something of the complexity which is America. As always, the programme had been prepared most imaginatively and understandingly. If I sometimes seemed depressed, you know the cause—it certainly had nothing to do with the programme.

> Much love,
> Indira

> Delegation of India to the 11th Session
> of the General Conference
> of UNESCO
> Paris
> December 4, 1960

Dorothy dear,

The passing away of a loved one, no matter how expected it may be, is always something of a shock and entails a whole series of mental and emotional adjustments. Life is made up of contacts with people—so that a separation, especially by something so final as death, leaves a void that no other person can fill. Still, this is a burden which each one of us must bear alone and one can only pray with Tagore "Let me not beg for the stilling of my pain, but for the heart to conquer it."

Your words, written or spoken, always have meaning—so don't hesitate to speak or write when you want to or for fear of misunderstanding. I don't think there can be that between us.

I am feeling much better—the fits of dark dark despair and depression do come but that is something I have always had—heaven knows when one looks around the world there is plenty to be depressed about! But on the whole I have got over that awful self-pity and preoccupation with my own sorrow.

My love and thoughts are with you.

Indira

Prime Minister's House
New Delhi
April 15, 1961

Dorothy dear,

You have already met Satish Gujral and have seen some of his paintings in our house. He is at present out on a world tour and is likely to be in New York soon. He has asked me to give him letters of introduction to people in New York. I cannot think of anybody except you although this seems a bit pointless as you seem to be in touch with all Indians who drift towards the U.S.

Gujral is a young painter who had spent some time

in Mexico and been greatly influenced by [José Clemente] Orozco's work. I have not seen his latest paintings but am told that he has now developed a style very much his own and has matured greatly. Our Consul General will know where to find Satish Gujral.

I am feeling so terribly depressed that I have not felt like writing and even this brief note dictated days ago has just been lying around. In the meantime your letter came yesterday. I am worried about so many things and since the last two days the heat is oppressive.

Mr. Galbraith[1] came to lunch yesterday. It's awfully good for the muscles just to look at him! Mrs. Galbraith seemed rather lost—it's a big change from a faculty wife to the U.S. Ambassador's Lady and I can imagine how everybody must be crowding in on her. However, she will soon find her footing.

I am off to Paris for UNESCO on the 21st or 22nd May until June 16th. Then to the International Union for Child Welfare June 19th to 22nd.

This afternoon I am going on a tour to Bombay, Hyderabad and Viyajawande—shall be back on the 26th April.

Lekha has been here.

Love,
Indira

1. John Kenneth Galbraith, United States Ambassador to India, 1961–1963.

Despite various invitations to make lecture tours in the United States, Indira never had time to accept them. Neither could she make contracts for the books about herself that several New York publishers asked her to write.

Dorothy dear,

I have been hesitating to write to you, waiting until I felt better. But now I really don't know if such a time will ever come. I've always thought of myself as a positive person. Now I feel terribly negative. I'm not ill. I'm not well. I just don't feel alive. Nobody seems aware of the difference! Do you think I have merely exhausted the supply of "mescaline" inside me? Pupul was here a couple of days ago, fresh and radiant from her five week Kashmir holiday. She advised me to do the same. I just can't. My second son is here alone. I am trying to settle him in a new school. As it is my time programme in India and abroad allows me very little time at home. If I did go off on my own I should not have any peace of mind.

My lecture tour in the United States had been fixed for the end of March onwards. In the meantime my father is going to Washington. Mr. Galbraith has extended a "personal invitation" to him. I am not clear what that means.

I have left my elder son Rajiv in school and he seems to be settling down well.

We are in the midst of the monsoons—Delhi is beautifully green but when the rain stops the humid heat becomes unbearable. In the South we have devastating floods. Politically the country is gathering momentum for the election.

With love,
Indira

Dorothy dear,

I have been in such a mad, mad rush—I can't remember whether I have written or not. I'm sorry my East African letter has got mislaid—it was straight from the heart, some glimmerings of excitement and reawakening.

Now I'm on my way to London—the plane is twelve hours late—I shall stay there at 9 Kensington Palace Gardens until the 24th October and then go to Paris for UNESCO. My father is expected in London on the 3rd or 4th November and we reach New York on the 5th. It will be good to see you.[1]

East Africa was exciting in many ways but depressing too. I am afraid my forebodings are coming true. My own mood has changed and I am in the depths of depression, for no special reason.

Have you finished your book?[2] Although I have been in the thick of things in India, I have a curious sense of isolation from everything—I hope I am more alive and awake by the time I get to the U.S.

With love,
Indira

1. President Kennedy had sent a formal invitation to Prime Minister Nehru and Indira to pay an official visit to the United States.
2. *Nehru: The First Sixty Years.*

During the 1961 trip to the United States by Nehru and Indira, I went to Washington to attend the major functions.

In New York, both Indira and Nehru were more eager

Indira with her parents, Kamala and Jawaharlal Nehru
Allahabad, about 1920

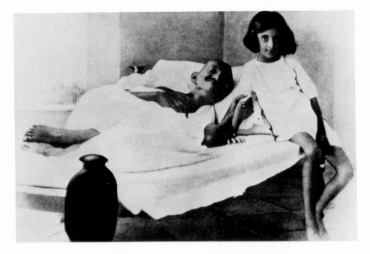

Indira with Mohandas K. Gandhi during one of his
fasts, New Delhi, 1924

Indira with her parents
Ceylon, early 1930s

Wedding of Indira and Feroze Gandhi
Allahabad, 1942

Room in Prime Minister Jawaharlal Nehru's official residence
New Delhi, 1950. Photograph by Dorothy Norman

President and Mrs. Ahmed Sukarno of Indonesia with
Jawaharlal Nehru and Indira Gandhi, New Delhi, 1950

Rajagopalachari, Dorothy Norman, and Indira Gandhi
(unidentified Indian woman, *right*), New Delhi, 1950

Indira Gandhi with her sons Rajiv *(left)* and Sanjay, New Delhi, 1950
Photograph by Dorothy Norman

Indira and Rajiv Gandhi, New Delhi, 1950
Photograph by Dorothy Norman

Indira Gandhi and Dorothy Norman
(unidentified Indian woman, *right*)
New Delhi, 1959

Indira Gandhi and James W. Symington,
U.S. Chief of Protocol, Langley
Air Force Base, Virginia, 1966

Indira Gandhi and Arthur Rubinstein, Washington, D.C., 1966

Indira Gandhi and Dorothy Norman, New York, 1983. Photograph
by Usha Bhagat

to go to the theatre than ever before. *We saw Laurence Oli-*
vier and Anthony Quinn in Jean Anouilh's Becket. *(Nehru*
asked me, upon hearing the name of the play, whether it
was by Tennyson.) He was amused by the scene about forks
having been introduced for the first time, since in Indian
villages hands are used for picking up food, rather than
Western cutlery.

Backstage after the performance we congratulated the
cast, and Nehru invited Olivier to visit him and Indira the
following day at his hotel. The distinguished actor arrived
in a dark brown suit, wearing glasses. He was unrecog-
nizable. At first everyone thought him to be a professor.

I took Indira to Henry Denker's A Far Country. *Be-*
cause it was about Freud's approach to psychoanalysis, I
thought it might interest her; it made a vivid impression.

Prime Minister's House
New Delhi
February 26, 1962

Dorothy dear,

I have just got back from a tour and seen your letter
of the 20th.

I was hoping that it would be possible for my elder
son, Rajiv, to come over to the United States, too, but he
can do this only if he can earn his way across. Some friends
have been finding out ways and means of doing this but
I do not yet know Rajiv's reaction.

I wonder whether either Pupul or Sahasrabudhe has
written to you. Everybody is impressed with him and I
think that the Children's Museum here is getting a move
on, though slowly.

Love,
Indira

In March 1962, Indira and Rajiv Gandhi stayed with
me in New York. Mary Lasker, who was in California, again
was helpful to Indira, when her American journey in-
cluded a trip to the West Coast.

Embassy of India
Washington, D.C.
March 26, 1962

Dorothy dear,

In spite of sleeping practically all the time, I have not
shaken off my fatigue and I am still feeling utterly utterly
exhausted. Heaven alone knows *how* I am going to survive this trip! The tiredness seems to reach deep inside
and I am so depressed!

It was so nice to see your dear familiar face. I wish I
had not been in such a daze. You are sweet to take so
much trouble. I am sorry to be relaying messages through
the Roys but my lack of energy prevents my taking any
action myself.

On the whole I feel it may be better to stay in New
York during the weekend. I do hope you don't mind. I
am quite vague about the programme. Did Sunil Roy tell
you that there is a possibility (rather remote, I'm afraid)
of Rajiv's coming over? I do hope he does.

Lots of love,
Indira

In flight
Los Angeles to Sacramento
April 4, 1962

Dorothy dear,

Your letter of March 29th was awaiting me in Los Angeles. Mary Lasker took me to lunch at Romanoff's. The [California] Attorney General (prompted by [Supreme Court] Justice [William O.] Douglas) gave a dinner at the Beverly Hilton (wonderful food) and the brothers of Lorraine Cooper[1] sent the most fabulous bouquet—pink roses and giant-size orchids. Nothing is lacking except me—I just don't know *where* I am. The body is there—grinning, talking, but it's just a shell. The real me is non-existent. Is it dead or dormant? It's *most* depressing and I miss me, if you know what I mean.

Sunil phoned Los Angeles and as usual I gave a message for you. Since I am feeling—or rather *not* feeling responsive to anything—I thought we had better stick to "light fare" at the theatre. I feel like a string instrument that's out of tune—the very sound of it grating to the ears.

Love,
Indira

1. Wife of U.S. Ambassador to India (1955–1956) John Sherman Cooper.

In flight to London
April 29, 1962

Dorothy dear,

Just a line to say thank you again—not merely for all the trouble you took, the arrangements, the giving of your time but really for the thought and the feeling underlying it all. I find it so moving that I am struck dumb and unable to say anything. The thing that bothers me is that although you do *so* much, you are constantly worrying whether it is enough or the right thing. For me it is enough to be with you. Other programmes are extras and sometimes "de trop."

Look after yourself and lots of love.

Indu

My two volumes on Prime Minister Nehru's First Sixty Years *were nearly completed in early September 1962. It was agreed that I should show him the unfinished manuscript in London. I received a message, on the day their plane was due, asking me to come at once to see Nehru, at the High Commissioner's Residence. I feared the trip would have tired Nehru, but carried the bulky pages with me in the event that he could look at them to see if there were errors.*

He appeared fresh; Indira, weary. He said to her, "Darling, you must go and rest." She did. After she left the room, he said, "Don't you think she looks terribly exhausted?" I concurred.

But the following day she looked fit and fresh. She begged me to go with her to see the film Lolita, *based on Vladimir Nabokov's novel. She loved it.*

Indira mistakenly expected me to be on hand when she returned to London in October; also to be in New York, where she was to make preliminary plans for the Indian Pavilion at the 1965 New York World's Fair. Unfortunately, I was traveling in Europe.

9 Kensington Palace Gardens
London W 8
October 7, 1962

Dorothy dear,

I don't know if this is going to reach you but I am writing anyway. I did a very silly thing—on your itinerary, I saw the date 6th and imagined it was October and that you would be in London today. What a disappointment to find that you are in Amsterdam.

The New York stay was MOST exhausting. I stayed with the Menons[1] who were very sweet and helpful. In fact if it had not been for the Menons, I don't think I could have done anything except for an informal dinner and get-together at the Asia Society and a meeting at the Community Church on October 2. Nothing was fixed and when I met people it was without any information regarding their background.

We have engaged Oscar Stonorov[2] and settled one or two other matters but a lot remains to be done. But I was so dead tired that I was just longing to get away.

Fortunately there was the opportunity to have a break. On arrival in London, I had a bath, quick lunch and I went off to Cambridge with Rajiv. Had two heavenly days. Quiet, restful, lovely weather, beautiful buildings.

But now I'm sad. It is rather a poignant moment, isn't it, for a mother when her child becomes a man and she knows that he is no longer dependent on her and that from now on he will lead his own life which she may or may not be allowed to glimpse. And even if she does sometimes look in, it can only be from outside, across the gap of a generation. New friendships, new attachments, new loves. My heart aches, but such is life. Not for nothing did our ancients leave all family attachments at a certain age and retire to meditate on the strangeness of the world and the Almighty. I wish I could—not necessarily meditate but retire anyway! As for Rajiv, I can only hope and pray that he will have the strength to face and accept life in all its varied facets.

I hope you are having a rewarding trip, making new discoveries and having a wonderful time.

Love,
Indira

1. Gopala Menon, Indian Consul General in New York.
2. Architect for the Indian Pavilion at the 1965 New York World's Fair.

Prime Minister's House
New Delhi
November 15, 1962

Dorothy dear,

I had promised to write to you in London but those were rather dreadful days and I just could not get a free moment. In the meantime your letter from London has come this morning. Thank you for it.

When we spoke on the phone I mentioned something about medical help. I was wondering whether some association or any foundation could help with some of the things of which we are in need.

The Defence Ministry and the Health Ministry both agree that one of the most urgent requirements is for plasma drying equipment as below.

Plasma Drying Equipment, Model L 80 P
  by Edwards High Vacuum, England
with a spin freezing machine and a 30 c. ft.
deep freezer to go with the above.

This becomes one Unit—four such Units are required.

The make mentioned above is English but there must be an American one too.

When I asked our Health Minister regarding this and other needs she took me at my word and has sent me an enormously long list but I cannot bother you with it at the moment, but would be glad if you could find out about the plasma drying equipment.

Would you advise me writing to someone else direct?

Pupul is here. Our plans for the Indian Pavilion have been drastically slashed but we are still participating.

Love,
Indira

In flight to Bombay
As at Prime Minister's House
New Delhi
May 21, 1963

Dorothy dear,

I found your letter awaiting me on my return from UNESCO in Paris. I always postpone writing to you because I feel that a hurriedly dictated letter is not good enough and that something more of me should go in. But somehow there never is the time to write that sort of letter and so, unfortunately, nothing at all is sent.

Even for me the schedule has been unbelievingly heavy since my return from the States, both before and after Paris, and there have been many nights when I have just not been able to go to bed at all. Once we returned home at 5:15 A.M. and had to leave for the airport at 6:30.

Even this letter is being dictated on a small plane which is taking me to Rajkot. I wonder if you know this town. This is a small one in Saurashtra but rather nice. My uncle, Ranjit Pandit, used to live there when he first married my aunt and I remember visiting them as a very small child and being overawed by the many hunting trophies which filled the house.

Unseasonable rains had brought a little coolness to Delhi the day I returned from Paris but now again it is very hot. We have some compensation in the form of the most beautiful flowering trees such as the golden laburnum and the most delicious fruit, such as mangoes and lichis.

As my father was not making up his mind about going to the hills, I decided to take Sanjay up to Almora which is quite a peaceful place with a most significant view of the snow-clad Himalayas. Almost the minute this had been more or less arranged my father announced his intention of going to Kashmir and since it cannot be fun for him to be alone while he is there, we will probably have to reorientate our own plans.

Love,
Indira

———————

Prime Minister's House
New Delhi
September 26, 1963

Dorothy dear,

I wonder if Pupul has already written to you. She did enjoy her visit to the U.S. because of Radhi[1] naturally but also because of her stay with you and the joy she has of working with you.

Our 1965 Worlds Fair Committee is most appreciative of the marvellous job you did in outlining the theme for the Indian Pavilion. We all fully applauded Pupul's idea that you should come out to India to help with the captions and we proposed this to the Ministry. However, the Ministry have not agreed, the reason as usual is finance, or rather LACK of it! We are all terribly sorry because you do have a natural aptitude . . . a gift for words. Your [book] *Heroic Encounter* is truly a joy forever. Every time one dips into it it reveals something new. It would have been good to have you in India.

Lack of money and this last minute rushing are creating many problems with the Indian Pavilion. Now that we see the scale model of the Pavilion, we find that the ramp takes up a lot of space and looks incongruous, especially on the ground floor, and we are trying frantically to see if this can be changed back to a staircase or escalator. We are terribly cramped for space and I just cannot figure out how everything will fit in. Much as we would have liked to we cannot even stick to the original theme because of lack of space. We have now to choose just a few of the more important ideas and try to express them in the best way possible.

At a time of life which is difficult in the best of circumstances I have been under tremendous physical and emotional strain, struggling with anaemia, low blood pressure, hormone imbalance—to mention only a few of my ills. Yesterday some intestinal infection was discovered which may well have caused the other conditions and for which I am now being treated.

I was due at the UNESCO meeting yesterday but find it impossible to get away and am now booked for the 29th night. However there is a possibility of certain important meetings here for which I may have to postpone my departure once more. The Executive Board meetings are to continue till the end of October but I doubt if I can stay beyond the middle of the month.

I am in the middle of another letter to you! It may follow in a couple of days.

Love,
Indira

1. Radhi Jayakar, Pupul's daughter.

Indira's desire for more privacy and for a new direction in her life was to be shattered by a multiplicity of unforeseeable events.

Prime Minister's House
New Delhi
October 13, 1963

Dorothy dear,

Your letter came yesterday. My promised letter is stuck halfway. I don't know when it can be completed.

This is purely personal. I have reached some kind of equilibrium at long last.

My need for privacy and anonymity has been growing steadily these last three years until now I feel I cannot ignore it without risking some kind of self-annihilation. Privacy, unfortunately, is not possible for me even in the remotest corner of this subcontinent. I have had people presenting their cards and their problems even at the foot of the Kolahoi glacier (16,000 ft. high)! It's not just meeting people but that they come only to get or ask something. And not even a few moments are left for thinking or relaxing or just being oneself.

Last May in London, I lost my heart to a small house

which was for sale. Such a wonderful location. Central, yet very quiet and next door to a park. If only I could have bought it! One room for myself and the rest (only two, I fear) rented out. Rents are so high and this would have solved the foreign exchange problem. But the major hurdle was the foreign exchange with which to buy it. I spent much time figuring out ways and means and finally when I learned that an acquaintance had bought it, I was terribly depressed for months. It was as if a door had been slammed in my face.

My father and sons have kept me tied to Delhi. Part of that problem is solved—Rajiv is in England and Sanjay finishes school by the end of the year. I should very much like him to go to England too. My living in London would make it easier for him to go abroad. And I would be able to see something of the boys and yet be on my own. Free to work or to rest. It doesn't sound much to ask of life yet it seems to be out of my reach. The only way out might be to get an adequate job—not under Indian government or business auspices.

Again, a couple of days ago, I spoke with Pupul. Her response was that I should talk with Krishnamurti[1] who is due in Delhi next month.

I am not running away from anybody or anything. I can claim to have done my duty to my country and my family all these long years. I don't for an instant regret it, because whatever I am today has been shaped by these years. But now I want another life. It may not work out. I may not like it or be good at it. But at least it deserves a trial. There is a compulsion within me which is driving me away from the old life. Is this wrong?

Love,
Indira

1. Indian philosopher and author.

During 1964, Jawaharlal Nehru's health deteriorated; it was difficult for him to admit it. For Indira, it was extremely upsetting to watch him fail.

Plans continued to be made, nonetheless, for the 1965 New York World's Fair, which required that Indira come to New York.

Prime Minister's House
New Delhi
January 4, 1964

Dorothy dear,

A very hurried line to acknowledge your letter of December 24th which I saw on my return a couple of days ago from a tour of some of the African countries.

I am so enmeshed in various problems that I have not even had a moment to look at correspondence much less to sort out my future programme. I shall write to you later about all this.

My thoughts have been very much with you, as going to a new place is always exciting and arouses new ideas which one wants to share.

The people with us were deadly dull and I felt most frustrated not being able to talk.

How I wish I could make a clean break with Indian or any other politics—I shall certainly try to.

Lots of love,
Indira

Orissa
January 10, 1964

Dorothy dear,

On my return from Africa at the end of December, I found Papu [Nehru] looking unwell. The programme he had fixed for himself for January was one that would have exhausted a young person of thirty. In fact, people who had seen merely the travel schedule said they could not have gone through with it. However, Papu fixes his programme on his own and then insists it is not possible to change any item.

There is nothing now to be done except for him to rest. It is sweet of you to want to help.

My father's illness is a mild one and as the doctors say, it's more like a "warning from nature." He must now be much more careful and strict about his schedule.

With love,
Indira

In flight from Udaipur
February 1, 1964

Dorothy dear,

I have had a brief interlude with the Pugwash Scientists.[1] Most interesting and stimulating. The Lake Placid Hotel is quite fabulous & ideal for such a conference—quiet and isolated yet so beautiful.

It was dear of you to offer to come. It was such a pleasant surprise to get your call—I tried to get a lot said in the fewest possible words. Hence the possibility of misunderstanding. Emotionally it is a help to be surrounded by friends but the physical conditions are often an obstacle. The nature of my responsibility is such that it cannot be shared. That is why I discourage friends.

My father is now well on the way to recovery and is already back to normal though he works at home. I want to delay the office-going for a while. The doctors say that had he been an ordinary person, they would have allowed him out long ago, but as he's P.M., they must be stricter!

There are tremendous pressures on me but I have managed to retain my balance so far! And certainly hope to continue to do so.

I shall try my best to come for the Fair but cannot yet name the dates or the duration of the stay.

With much love,
Indira

1. The Pugwash conferences were founded by industrialist Cyrus Eaton to study the effects—negative and positive—of recent scientific discoveries.

Prime Minister's House
New Delhi
April 3, 1964

Dorothy dear,

This is my usual hurried note—hardly entitled to be called a letter. Pupul must have told you how harassed we all are. We seem to live from crisis to crisis and, as if the international, national and domestic troubles were not enough, I have got a slipped disk as well. I am encased in an unlovely plastic collar, which is terribly uncomfortable and hot.

I hope you will be in New York when I am there. I

decided to stay at the Menons' but only because I was in such bad humor that I did not wish to inflict it on any one else.

The stay in New York [to plan the Indian Pavilion] is terribly short but I hope Sunil will leave some time free for us to meet.

Love,
Indira

———————————

Prime Minister's House
New Delhi
April 14, 1964

Dorothy dear,

A thousand apologies for not writing to you. Perhaps Pupul would have given some indication of why. It hasn't anything to do with you—just the world in general—and myself in particular. I have done only those letters which were thrust on me.

Travelling has become a terrible burden what with the rush before going when one is racing against time, and the rush when one gets there. I hate long trips and get utterly exhausted.

You will probably know more about my programme than I know myself since Sunil and Bijju are drawing it up. I had written to Sunil to be sure to leave time for you and hope he has given you this message.

As the programme stands I am due to leave New York on the 24th, returning on the 27th. Without telling anybody I had been looking forward to spending a couple of days very quietly there, especially to have the opportunity of talking with you. Since last night plans have changed again and I must return back here as soon as possible. In fact if President Johnson's appointment has not been fixed for the 27th I would have left before. Now I shall fly back direct to India without stopping anywhere. Dreadfully tiring journey.

Sunil mentions *Dr. Strangelove*[1]—I expect you've seen it and everything else that is to be seen. If you have the time, perhaps Pupul, you and I could [do] something together.

Meanwhile this brings my warmest love.

Indira

1. The film, directed by Stanley Kubrick.

———————

BOAC In flight
Frankfurt-Rome
April 28, 1964

Dorothy dear,

How very frustrating it was to see you and go away almost immediately. Anyway it was good to know that you are very much better. I hope you will soon be quite well again. I may come again. I should like to. But one just doesn't know. I was at London airport for only about fifteen minutes. Rajiv had come down but of course there was no time for anything but a hasty peck on the cheek!

Isn't it fascinating, how living half a world away, with entirely different times and environment, we should have so much in common and share the same ambitions?

I hope some day there will be more time to talk at "leisure." This is the age of leisure and yet more and more people, like us, seem to have less and less of it. In India I am so tensed up and even if there is time I cannot really unwind.

Pupul was radiant with her success. She has done a wonderful job with the ground floor of our Pavilion in Rome and on the administrative side. We are now trying to change the first floor [of the New York Pavilion] and make it more interesting and imaginative. We have all missed you tremendously.

Lots of love,
Indira

———————

Prime Minister's House
New Delhi
May 8, 1964

Dorothy dear,

The whole question of my future is bothering me. I feel I must settle outside India at least for a year or so and this involves earning a living and especially foreign currency. This isn't just yet but it is a nagging worry. The desire to be out of India and the malice, jealousies and envy, with which one is surrounded, are now overwhelming. Also the fact that there isn't one single person to whom one can talk or ask advice even on the lesser matters.

Keep well.

Love,
Indira

———————

Prime Minister Jawaharlal Nehru's death in May 1964 represented a sad moment for the Indian people and a special tragedy for Indira Gandhi.

A Memorial Exhibition honoring him was to be held in New York in 1965. Indira and Pupul Jayakar suggested that I come to India to help work on it, but plans continually changed.

Prime Minister's House
New Delhi
June 11, 1964

My dear Dorothy,

Thank you for message [about Nehru's death]. Personal grief is so minute a part of the void which he has left.

He burnt with a "gemlike flame." How can I believe that it can go out? I feel his presence all round and pray that it may always be so.

I have received so many letters of warm sympathy from all over the world from people who knew and loved him. Yours brings me special comfort for I know you share our sorrow in a deeply personal way.

Yours sincerely,
Indira

Teen Murti House
New Delhi
July 5, 1964

Dorothy dear,

This is to send you my love and to apologise for not writing earlier. You can well imagine what tremendous strain I have been through and it is not over yet. I am feeling utterly exhausted, physically, mentally and emotionally. Your letters meant a great deal to me and I did want to write, but somehow no words came.

What has happened is that all the acknowledgements to strangers have gone off, but special friends have been left out because I felt that I should write myself but found myself unable to do so.

In the meantime, I have got involved in a number of things. This is too complicated to write about and I do not know how it is going to work out. But if you believe in stars, my stars must be against my plans for myself!

What I really wanted to tell you now is that the Government is planning an exhibition on my father to be shown in New York and perhaps simultaneously in India and other countries also. We are having the usual trouble regarding planning and execution. I should be very grateful for your ideas and help. My own idea is that we should try to show him as the "complete" man that he was. The thread that should run through historical and other aspects is that of his deep compassion which was responsible for bringing him into public life and for the policies which he pursued; and secondly, his astonishing courage which enabled him to fight for his policies and achieve a large measure of success.

The method of working which I have suggested to the people here is to select captions from his own writings or speeches which would bring out these aspects and then to choose the pictures to suit the captions. There will also perhaps be films and use of recordings of his voice. This is a brief outline. I am sure you will be able to put more meaning into it. I had asked Usha to write to you about this and it is only today that I learnt that she has not done so.

Pupul has arrived back and we have also discussed this matter. I was hesitating to bring you in, knowing how busy you were with your book.

Pupul is anxious that this undertaking should be given over to the Design Institute. But for some reason Government is a little allergic to this but is willing to engage an American display artist. Do you have any suggestions?

Dorothy, I have had my share of sorrow but what I feel now is something so much deeper, permeating my whole being. Grief and sorrow are wholly inadequate words to describe it. At the same time I feel him [Nehru] close.

I have so much work, I can't think how I am going to survive!

With much love,
Indira

P.S. Shall be at Claridge's until the 15th or 16th. If I stay in London longer, I shall move to the High Commission or somewhere.

After Nehru's death, Lal Bahadur Shastri became India's second Prime Minister.

Although Indira Gandhi had shunned taking office in 1964, she later agreed to be Minister for Information and Broadcasting under Shastri.

Minister
Information and Broadcasting
India
July 27, 1964

My dear Dorothy,

The work on the [Nehru] Exhibition is being done in India. But since many photographs, films, and other material may be available in the States, we had asked our

Embassy in Washington to help in collecting them. At this end, a Committee had been formed, of which I was not a member. But, as you know, this does not stop me from putting my foot in if I consider it necessary! This Committee is a very small one and has mostly concerned itself with choosing a theme for the Exhibition.

Our Principal Information Officer has collected a large number of photographs. The question now is to choose which we want and also to have the right captions. My own idea was to choose the write-ups, as far as possible, in my father's own words and then to match the pictures. We all feel that you would be the best person to do this and we would be most grateful if you could pay a brief visit to India as soon as you can, preferably in August, as time is extremely limited.

With love,
Indira

Indira came to the United States for the opening of the Nehru Memorial Exhibition; we were asked to speak about it on the same television program. The Indian Ambassador to the United Nations invited us to see Fiddler on the Roof *in the evening.*

In private, we shared our grief about Nehru's death and poured our hearts out to one another, as always.

1, Safdarjang Road
New Delhi
December 20, 1964

Dorothy dear,

I have just come back from Burma—an extraordinary

trip about which I shall tell you later. As I had no news of you, I wrote to Fory from Burma asking her to find out whether I could stay with you. So I am naturally happy to have your letter. I would love to be with you regardless of the service.

As regards the programme [for the Nehru Memorial Exhibition], I myself have not got much idea. Fory will be better informed.

I am glad to hear about the [Nehru] book. Your Indian publisher had requested an introductory note from our President and the Prime Minister. The President has sent a good one. I do not think Shastriji has replied yet.

With much love,
Indira

New York
January 28, 1965

Dorothy dear,

I am writing this in the car, so my writing will be even more illegible than usual.

The morning has been a hectic rush—telegrams from India needing replies and so on, otherwise I would have telephoned.

The first thing I want to say is that you were looking quite enchantingly beautiful. This is the first time I have seen you in white—how well it suits you.

I, on the other hand, was feeling and looking ghastly. I don't know how I got through the evening—didn't get home until 12:30 a.m. Now I am on my way to the airport. I haven't had a chance to pack, or think of my speeches or anything. I wanted very much to come to you on the 30th straight from the airport but that will not be possible now as my belongings are strewn all over the place at the Carlyle. So this is what we have decided.

We shall pick you up in the morning on our way to the Exhibition for the T.V. I shall then return home with you and if it is convenient, shall lunch and have dinner with you on the 31st. On the 30th I seem to have got tied up with appointments. If there is a moment, I shall drop in or at least phone. Anyway we are all looking forward to seeing you at dinner and the theatre.

When I come back on the 2nd, I shall stay a while close to the airport. But I shall call you again on the 5th.

Wasn't the Exhibition good?

Much love,
Indira

The Carlyle
New York
January 31, 1965

Dorothy,

Isn't it wonderful how the years vanish when we meet and the conversation flows as if the interruption had been one of a day or so?

This is just to send my love—

Indu

Minister
Information and Broadcasting
New Delhi
May 31, 1965

My dear Dorothy,

The functions which were held on the 27th and 28th went off very well.[1] In the morning of the 27th, we had prayers from 5:00 to 5:30 and later from 5:30 to 6:30 Shrimati M. S. Subbalakshmi[2] sang some bhajans.[3] She sang most beautifully and the atmosphere was just as we had wanted it, full of peace and beauty.

I did not go to any of the Government programmes. These were a military salute at Shanti Vana[4] at 8:00 A.M. and a public meeting at 6:30 P.M. The Education Ministry had at the suggestion of the Memorial Committee organized a symposium in Vigyan Bhavan.[5] At night, there was a symposium on AIR.[6]

On the 27th from 7:30 to 11:45 P.M. we had five of our top musicians—Ravi Shankar, Ali Akbar Khan, Vilayat Khan, Gopala Krishnan and Narayanaswami—playing at Shanti Vana. This was not intended as a concert but merely so that people who came to pay homage could do so in peace and beauty. Many people had doubts about the success of this as the average man is not known for his love of classical music. However, it went off extremely well, the huge crowd moving around quietly and a considerable number sitting and listening to the music. I myself had thought that I would go there for a short while and come away. But once there it was impossible to move and I sat until the end. It was 11:45 P.M. It seemed to me that I had never heard these musicians play so sweetly—particularly Ali Akbar Khan—who was the last—especially excelled himself.

On the 28th evening, towards the time of his cremation, we had a symbolic tree-planting ceremony by the children of Bal Bhavan. It was not publicized. There was the normal Shanti Vana crowd, two hundred fifty children from Bal Bhavan, Shastriji and myself. It was done in Santiniketan style—children singing Hindi translations of Gurudev's [Tagore's] songs, walking in procession some with cymbals and others with branches, girls with decorated earthenware pots of water, small boys with digging implements. Four boys carried what looked like a palanquin of flowers. This held the saplings to be planted. Everything went off well and I think was a fitting end to the ceremonies of the two days.

With love,
Indira

1. Ceremonies in observance of the first anniversary of Nehru's death.
2. Leading exponent of Indian classical music and dance.
3. Musical composition of a devotional nature.
4. Site of Nehru's cremation.
5. Major site in New Delhi for national and international meetings of scientists and political leaders.
6. All India Radio.

1, Safdarjang Road
New Delhi
March 11, 1965

Dorothy dear,

Your letter has come and also one from Max Reinhardt about your [Nehru] book. But the book has not reached me yet.

We are in the midst of our Budget Session of Parliament and we are busier than ever. On top of this, there are many crises—real or imaginary—so that there is an uproar in Parliament every day. The situation is frustrating and demoralising in many ways and yet it is not as bad as the press makes it out to be. Mr. Shastri, I think, is feeling stronger now and more sure of himself.

The Indian edition of the book has just come.

Much love,
Indira

Dorothy dear,

Guess who's here? Mary Lord and her husband. They are on their way to Japan, then via Trans Siberian Railway to Outer Mongolia to look for wild animals!!

Rajiv and I are up here for the coronation.[1] It's colorful and gay. The arrangements for so many guests in such a tiny spot are truly wonderful. But it is all terribly unusual and seems so unconnected with this world.

How is your leg now? I have been having ups and downs and mostly downs.

I think of you so often—no time to write and difficult to express or rather to commit to paper, all that one would like to say. Am longing for a real holiday in the mountains.

Much love,
Indira

1. Of the Chogyal of Sikkim.

Minister
Information and Broadcasting
New Delhi
November 5, 1965

My dear Dorothy,

Knowing your deep concern for the success of our family planning programmes, I am writing to you for your advice. We have two problems:

1. As you know, there are a large number of family planning clinics and information regarding family planning is being given by many hospitals. But the most effective medium of publicity is through radio. Unfortunately only a fraction of the broadcasting potential is being utilized. Less than three-fourths of the population can now receive broadcasts on medium wave and in the rural areas listening is confined mostly to community receivers provided by the Central and State Governments. A sample survey on rural farm broadcasting in the Punjab done by the FAO some time ago showed that our programmes have been fairly effective.

My Ministry is anxious to get about two millon low-cost radio receivers so that our rural programmes and programmes on family planning could reach all parts of the country. I have written to FAO and UNESCO to find out whether we could get any assistance from them in getting cheap radio sets which our farmers could afford.

2. With the help of the Government of West Germany, we have expanded our experimental Delhi Television Centre. Apart from educational programmes during school hours, we have an hour's daily show of entertainment and social education programmes. All the TV sets at present are either in schools or community tele-clubs and a few in hospitals. Some are being put up for sale to the public. All this is in New and Old Delhi. However, we find that the TV range also extends to six hundred villages, out of which over three hundred have electricity. I feel that this is a wonderful opportunity to try out programmes of better farming methods as well as family planning through TV, since the visual impact is so much greater than the spoken word. We are trying to persuade village panchayats[1] to buy TV sets. Due to the extreme shortage of foreign exchange, it is not possible for Government to import more at the present moment. It would

naturally expedite matters if we could have help on this from any organization interested in family planning or in increased agricultural production.

Since you yourself are greatly interested in these matters and are in touch with Trusts and other bodies which may be able to help, I thought I should write to you.

I have also written to C. V. Narasimhan[2] as during his visit to India just over a year ago he showed great interest and urged me to take up family planning publicity in a big way.

Good wishes,
Indira

1. Village council or court consisting of five elected, wise elders.
2. Of the U.N. Secretariat.

Prime Minister's House
New Delhi
March 1, 1966

Dorothy dear,

Thank you for your letter and cable.[1] I am sorry for the delay in acknowledging them but you can imagine the rush I have been in.

How like you, your letters are full of warmth. You know how I value your friendship and good wishes.

There is so much to be said but just no time for more.

With good wishes and love,

Yours,
Indira

1. Sent to congratulate Indira when she became Prime Minister.

President Lyndon B. Johnson invited Indira Gandhi,
India's new Prime Minister, to come to the United States
on an official visit in December 1966. There were the usual
banquets, official talks and interviews. While still in
Washington, she attended a dinner in her honor hosted by
the B. K. Nehrus. Johnson came to the preliminary recep-
tion and, ignoring all protocol, remained, uninvited, for
dinner. He wore his daily business attire, whereas every-
one else was in evening clothes. It proved to be an extraor-
dinary occasion, a real tribute to Mrs. Gandhi. (India was,
in fact, in need of much aid at the time.) In New York, the
Asia Society held a gala banquet for her.

Prime Minister's House
New Delhi
March 10, 1966

Dorothy dear,

Your letter of the 4th arrived yesterday. Naturally I
shall be delighted to see you. But the programme at the
moment is very rushed, and I do not know how anything
can be fitted in. I wish they had arranged something relaxing, but there does not seem to be much hope for that.
Do come to Washington if you can.

With love,
Indira

Prime Minister's House
New Delhi
May 27, 1966

Dorothy dear,

You are one of my morale builders so I was naturally delighted to get your letter. You have been so much in my thoughts. There is so much to say that one does not know where to begin.

This will give you an idea of my programme. A couple of days ago I returned from Bombay. It was a hectic visit. We had the All India Congress meetings there—these were held in a hall ten miles from Raj Bhavan[1] where I was staying. I had to do the journey four times a day, and every day whether it was a holiday or not, in the hot sunshine or late at night there were people, six to eight deep every inch of the way and I had to stand and wave. No one has seen such crowds since the early days of independence. It was the same in Poona but on a lesser scale as Poona is so much smaller.

In Poona in the morning I visited the drought affected areas, several irrigation schemes, held a couple of meetings and so on. It was terribly hot and dusty. In the afternoon I visited the military hospitals and rehabilitation centres for disabled jawans.[2] In the evening there was a reception and a public meeting.

The next day I flew to Mahabaleshwar[3] to see a training programme, flew back to Poona and on to Delhi. Mahabaleshwar is quite delightful and I wished I could have stayed on for a day.

Much love,
Indira

1. Governor's Residence.
2. Soldiers of the Indian Army.
3. Hill station in Maharashtra State.

116

Prime Minister's House
New Delhi
February 10, 1967

Dorothy dear,

Ever since plastic surgery was heard of I have been wanting to get something done to my nose. I even started putting by money for it and I thought the only way it could be done without the usual hoo-ha was first to have some slight accident which would enable me to have it put right—but—as you know, things never happen the way one wants them to. You must have heard that at my meeting in Bhubaneshwar there was some pebble throwing. There were just a few students who had grouped themselves in a circle, standing, jumping, and shouting slogans. They were surrounded by a huge gathering [of people] who were quietly listening and would every now and then burst out in a "Jai" [Victory].

I gave my full speech, about forty to forty-five minutes, but while I was speaking I knew they must be throwing stones or something because the Press people who were below the dais looked alarmed and moved behind the dais.

When I finished speaking people wanted me to sit behind while somebody got up for the vote of thanks. I thought it was important that I should be right in front so I stayed and got a large piece of brick right on my face. There was a spurt of blood—I thought at first that my nose was broken. Someone gave me a handkerchief. I wanted to stay till the meeting ended but after a little while the idea struck me that if something is broken it should be set immediately so I went home. The meeting went on for quite a while afterwards.

In Raj Bhavan I found that I looked like a boxer—I

was a terrible sight in the mirror. My nose, the left side, looked completely crooked. As it was I tried to put it right myself and heard a little "tik" sound. The left lip had swollen to the size of a big egg. Most of my face was also discoloured and I bled for quite a while through the nose.

Orissa is so disorganized that it took a lot of time for even the doctors to come and then there was a lengthy argument as I said my nose was fractured and they said it was not. Thanks to my own common sense, I kept ice on my face all the time and brought down the swelling.

I kept to my programme and spoke at a huge meeting in Patna next morning and then came here. After examination they find the left nasal bone which was cracked is slightly displaced and I am now at the Willingdon Hospital where it will be set right. Although the swelling has almost gone I am still looking awful.

11th February

You should see me now, with an impressive crepe bandage on my forehead and my nose banded across.

Usha chooses just this moment—as I came out of the anaesthesia—to read out the gruesome story of the Kennedy assassination.[1] It is very well written and is gripping—just the thing to read in a hospital.

I had to "re-do" the room because an artist, who was in the hospital some time ago, had donated his grimmest pictures here, and the one in my room was of a ghastly gnarled old tree, dominating the room. It has now been put in the back verandah and the room is quite cheerful.

With love,
Indira

1. An article containing allegedly new findings about the 1963 assassination of President Kennedy.

Djakarta
July 2, 1967

Dear Dorothy,

Each trip to a country gives a new insight. Isn't it fascinating how people are different and yet the same? The women of Indonesia—the young ones!—are like dolls, quite exquisite.

With love,
Indira

In 1968 Indira came to New York City for a brief visit.

The Carlyle
New York
October 13, 1968

Dorothy dear,

How good it was to see you again. I was sorry there was such a rush—it got worse and worse until about 9:30 and then suddenly everyone was gone. I watched Channel 13 for a while. Usha is shopping and it is quiet.

New York is a city which grows on one. London used to be my favorite but I have switched my loyalty ro New York I think. The view from each side of this suite is quite different and each very lovely.

This is just to send my love and to thank you and to say how much I miss our talks. Talking to you is like loud thinking and makes me think clearer!

Keep well.

Love,
Indu

P.S. I had closed the envelope when Usha told me that you had rung up at 11—just when I was writing to you!

———————

Prime Minister's House
New Delhi
April 30, 1969

Dorothy dear—
How are you? We have had no news for a long time. We are all well and busy—more than usual and with crises of one kind or another. The summer has begun. Delhi is ablaze with the colors of flowering trees.

Love,
Indu

———————

Prime Minister's House
New Delhi
May 26, 1969

Dorothy dear,
Your letter of the 12th has just arrived. How I wish you would come for a short time, perhaps in the winter, which is so nice in Delhi. We have a tiny guest room but you will always be welcome to stay in it.

Your Mr. [William] Rogers[1] was here. He is charming and seems to be understanding. I do hope we can make a fresh start with the new administration. Mr. Rogers said that Ambassador [Kenneth] Keating[2] is a close friend of the President and is also popular in Congress and that he himself asked to come to India as Ambassador. This is a good sign. Ambassador Keating was here for Dr. Zakir Husain's[3] funeral. I met him briefly. He seemed a nice person. The Bowles[4] are sweet, as you know, but he had become very old and unwell.

I am afraid it is my fault that Rajiv and Sonia [his Italian wife] have not written to thank you for the records, which they like very much and are enjoying. Although I had told them that you had sent them, I forgot to mention that they were a wedding present to them. They have asked me to thank you.

Apart from being beautiful, Sonia is a really nice girl, wholesome and straightforward. Perhaps you know that Rajiv is working with the Indian Airlines.

Guess who turned up here the other day? Our old friend Bucky Fuller. He is as young and forward-looking as ever. He has paid me the biggest compliment and I must share it with you. On one of his maps, he has inscribed as follows: "To Indira, in whose integrity God is entrusting much of the evolutionary success of humanity and with utter safety." I must say I was deeply touched and also somewhat embarrassed.

With much love,
Indira

P.S. We both thank you very much.
Rajiv   Sonia

1. U.S. Secretary of State.
2. Former U.S. Senator from New York and U.S. Ambassador to India, 1969–1972.
3. President of India, 1967–1969.
4. Chester Bowles, U.S. Ambassador to India, 1951–1953 and 1963–1969.

In flight
Srinagar to Delhi
September 4, 1969

Dorothy dear,

I have just been on a 3½ days holiday to Gulmarg, in Kashmir. I can't remember when I last had a holiday. I have wallowed in idleness, gone riding in the hills and walking in the woods. Reading odd things, amongst them Voznesensky's[1] *Antiworlds.* "Some one's beating a woman. But her light is unfaltering. World without ending. There are no religions, no revelations, there are women."!

What utter nonsense the press is putting out—especially our own. Some of yours—Max Lerner[2] and the *New York Times*—are nearer the mark than much that is appearing here. Need I assure you that I am *not* closer to the communists or to dictatorship of any kind. The communists, as indeed any political party, will certainly try to exploit the situation for their own ends. This can only be prevented by our own vigilance and by tackling basic problems. I am more and more convinced that the people will support the Congress if they can be led to hope that the Congress is on their side. Unfortunately the institution of bossism created a clash between the party and the people as a whole. Each state boss came to believe that he *was* the state. This is what I have tried to break through. Perhaps because I have tried to be accommodating, they all thought I was weak. These last two years have been of tremendous pressure and difficulty. If it had been a question of myself or my position, it would not have mattered but the manner in which I was being pushed around, with a view to finally pushing me out of office, would certainly have not only split the Congress but weakened it all along the line. The Communists have been able to come to power in West Bengal and Kerala, because of the split in the State Congress. In both cases this was avoidable and I had pleaded with the then Congress president, but the opinion of the local (or State) Boss prevailed.

I do not know what the future holds—there is no doubt of travail and difficulty but there is a new enthusiasm in the entire country and the possibility that we may be able to use it to our advantage. That is the only hope for India's stability. Far from weakening democracy we have strengthened it.

Shall write later. Must rush, the latter part of this letter was written in Delhi just before leaving for another journey.

Love,
Indira

1. Russian poet Andrei Voznesensky.
2. American journalist and author.

In flight to Cochin
December 15, 1969

Dorothy dear,

I had meant to write along with the Christmas card but before I could do so, it had been sent off.

You're always bragging about the joys and the "superior status" of being a grandmother, so I thought I should let you in on the secret and let you know that I am competing too. Sonia is expecting a baby toward the end of April. Isn't it exciting? Although when one's daughter-in-law is from another continent, there are many complexities too.

I am on my way to Cochin to celebrate the 400th anniversary of the synagogue. I had made this engagement before becoming the P.M.! It is a long journey—2745 miles taking 7½ hrs including two short breaks in Bangalore to change planes—all in a day. Couldn't take more time off because of Parliament.

My thoughts are with you.

Much love,
Indira

Part Three

THE SEVENTIES AND EIGHTIES

My dear Dorothy,

Your book[1] indeed is the most beautiful one from the point of view of presentation as well as what is in it. I have not been able to do more than glance at it. I have been almost constantly on tour. Although I do take reading material on tour, I did not want to take this as moving about from plane to helicopter and helicopter to car might spoil the book. However, I do want to let you know how delighted I am to have it. I have no doubt that it will help to give a new dimension to my thinking which is so necessary when one is involved in such fast moving political events.

My thoughts are often with you and sometimes I plan long letters but due to lack of time they do not get written. I have not written to Bucky Fuller either. Perhaps he has shown you the long letter of gratitude which he has written to me.

With love,
Indira

1. *The Hero—Myth, Image, Symbol.*

Prime Minister
New Delhi
August 22, 1970

Dorothy dear,
Your brief notes are always welcome morale boosters. Our talks, though brief and far between, have had depth. A conversation with an understanding and discerning person helps one to clarify one's own thoughts.

My grandson, Rahul,[1] is a darling. He has got rid of his wrinkles and still has his double chin!

With love and greetings,
Indira

1. Rajiv and Sonia Gandhi's son.

September 4, 1970

Dorothy dear,
Do you know [Indian poet] P. Lal's books? The two

hymns I love are "To the Unknown God" and "The Song of Creation."

Much love,
Indira

In 1971, Indira Gandhi was reelected Prime Minister, and was confronted by the horrifying results of Pakistan's repressive attempts to put down the uprising in East Pakistan.

The Retreat
Mashobra (Simla Hills)
April 23, 1971

Dorothy dear,

I find I have not replied to various messages from you. The telegram after the news of the plane mishap in Orissa. Is it not strange that something happens every time I go to Orissa? This particular incident was nothing much. I have had a worse experience some years ago, when one of the engines of a Dakota actually burst into flames.

Then there was your cable and letter about the election results.

I have delayed writing to you as I was awaiting the chance of writing a longer letter. But you know how difficult this is, even when one is on holiday. There is a pile of work and I have never been less in a holiday mood. I think it was [poet Stephen] Spender who said that to take a holiday was a state of mind, not the travelling to a particular place. Right now we are staying beyond Simla in a house which used to be a week-end retreat for the Viceroy and now belongs to the President. I have been here several times with my father or the children, but nobody else has used it since the Mountbattens left. The house is very English countryside in character with some lovely old tables and other things. It is quiet and you know how much I love the mountains. There are several mountain ranges and behind them the eternal snows.

The elections have already slipped into history. We did expect a big majority. What was exhilarating was the manner in which many people and especially the younger generation of all sections made our election campaign their own. Perhaps you will be interested to read a brief note I sent to a friend in England. I enclose a copy.

Thank you for the books which came just as I was leaving for Mashobra. I brought them along but have not had a moment to do more than glance at them.

Much love,
Indira

[Enclosure]

Newspapers here and abroad have, as usual, missed the essential point about these elections. They have highlighted the oddities but ignored the over one hundred fifty million who voted. The question is not one of the majority. What has been extraordinary and exhilarating is that the elections became a sort of movement—a people's movement. Thus, from village after village we got news that when our sympathizers went to campaign, they were stopped at the entrance and asked for whom they stood. If they took my name, they were welcomed—often with brass bands and sweets! or told that the village vote was solid for us and therefore they need not waste their time. Taxi drivers and scooter rickshaw drivers not only offered the use of their vehicles free but themselves paid for the petrol. These are only a few examples. The peasant, the worker and, above all, the youth cut across all caste, religious and other barriers to make this their own campaign with tremendous enthusiasm. In Delhi, large numbers of people who had regular jobs and who worked in offices, factories or elsewhere in the daytime came to our office afterwards and worked until two and three in the morning for nearly a month on a purely voluntary basis. Our party does not have paid campaign workers.

Two days after the results were announced, an acquaintance was in search of a taxi and was surprised to find no response from any of the nearby stands. Finally she came down herself and located a solitary cab but the driver refused to take her, saying that they had all been celebrating the victory and were a bit high and since she seemed to be a good sort, he would not advise her to take a taxi in that area on that particular night!

There are many such stories involving different sections of people.

While the rural and urban populations were attracted by our economic programme—there is no doubt that the young people and intelligentsia supported our modern outlook. All sections were repelled by the campaign of hate and vilification concentrated against me.

I was astonished to read in some foreign papers that our party—the New Congress—had the most material resources. Actually, with the exception of the CPI [Communist Party of India] and PSP [People's Socialist Party], we had the least—our resources were made up of fairly small donations from the small and middle industrialists and the general public. Ranged against us was the "grand alliance" of several parties, supported financially and otherwise by the big industrialists and the princes, etc. One of our M.P.s from Bihar who has been elected against all expectations because his area was the stronghold of a prince whose family had dominated the scene in the last elections, says that his opponent lost in proportion to the money he spent and the abuses he hurled at me!

By and large, writers, artists, lawyers, teachers, etc. supported our party. But strong opposition came from columnists and leader [editorial] writers of big national papers all of which are owned by big industrial families. Their opposition to our policies is not new, since they had also opposed my father throughout his Premiership.

In the forty-three days at my disposal, I travelled over thirty-six thousand miles, addressed over three hundred meetings. The official estimate is that about thirteen million people attended my meetings and another seven million lined the roads. It was wonderful to see the light in their eyes. By the way, in all this travel except in some districts and in some tribal Harijan (ex-untouchables) groups, nowhere did I see the sort of poverty which was so prevalent twenty years ago. Whether they had proper shelter and clothing or not, almost everywhere the children were healthy and bright-eyed.

Prime Minister's House
New Delhi
August 29, 1971

Dorothy dear,

This is just to warn you that I will be turning up in the United States. The rough dates are as follows:

November 3rd, 4th and 5th in Washington
November 5th afternoon and 6th in New York.

As usual, there is hardly any time. But it was this or nothing at all. I am asking Usha to keep in touch with you. If at all possible, I should like to have the same sort of get together I had the last time. But I would not like you to take the trouble. If you could phone and let L. K. Jha[1] know, I am sure he will do the needful.

Until the news is announced it is confidential.

Love,
Indira

1. Indian Ambassador to the United States.

The Carlyle
New York
November 7, 1971

Dorothy dear,

You reminded me last night of the first time we had met—I saw something, a rare quality—in your face and asked you for your photograph. Through the years your friendship has meant much to me. In a way, one uses all one's experiences and even one's friends to grow on. I have grown and you have played a considerable part in my growth.

Except for those few days when I came after my kidney operation, we haven't ever had the time to talk. Yet in some mysterious and inexplicable way we have kept in touch.

This is just to send my love. Keep well and be yourself.

Nancy and your son Andrew are so good-looking, not just the first look but deep down.

Love,
Indira

Dorothy dear,

Our letters have probably crossed.

What can I say about myself? During this trip [to the United States] I was reminded of a story I read long ago. Some domestic circumstance compelled a sophisticated young woman to take home with her a middle-class, middle-aged suburban aunt. The feeling of guilt at leaving the aunt alone overcame the worry over any likely embarrassment and she was taken out to meet the young set. The urban sophisticates were so unaccustomed to naturalness, directness and honest to goodness truth that she gained a reputation for wit and wisdom. A young designer said that she was not expressing her personality and re-designed her wardrobe in bright colors and new shapes which were then unknown. So she became a big hit and was in great demand in society!

Substitute "woman P.M." for "new wardrobe" and it could be me!

You have probably heard that Pupul has had a cardiac insufficiency. I was astonished to hear that she wanted to come to greet me on my birthday and tried to put her off for her own sake, but she insisted. She was emotional about me and also I think about herself, for this illness must have given a jolt to her—such an active person that she is.

With love,
Indira

During Indira's 1971 visit to New York, I arranged a gathering for her that was typical of other informal meetings I had organized at her request. A cross-section of writers, editors, and artists had come together to discuss with her advanced trends of thought in the United States. The intent was to have guests answer any questions she might have. This time, however, the tensions of the moment between East and West Pakistan occupied everyone's thoughts.

The central government of Pakistan was waging hostilities against the uprising in East Pakistan. As a result, some ten million East Pakistanis were crossing India's border, which meant she must feed and give refuge to them. The situation had become so grave that no one seemed interested in talking about anything else. Indira was besieged by queries about what the United States could do to help. Whether Hannah Arendt asked, or Edward Albee, Erik Erikson or John Cage, the intensity was identical.

India soon went to war against Pakistan to end the violence in East Pakistan. She was victorious and called for a cease-fire. East Pakistan became Bangladesh.

Indira was ever eager to hear music in New York. We attended a performance of the New York Philharmonic Orchestra, conducted by Leonard Bernstein. I bought tickets for George Balanchine's New York City Ballet. At the last moment, Indira said she could not join me. I showed my surprise; she looked unnerved and sad. I could not understand what had happened; we had spoken of how we looked forward especially to a new Stravinsky ballet. Indira commented only, "I can't go. It will be too wonderful. I won't be able to bear it." She was on the verge of tears. In the morning she had regained her equilibrium.

Prime Minister
Cochin
April 29, 1972

Dearest Dorothy,

Just to send you my love.

If at all there is a good God presiding over our destinies, I think He is excessively occupied in thinking up problems for India to solve! No sooner is one crisis over, than something else is looming over the horizon. Success brings its own responsibilities and also evokes jealousies. This year is going to be a testing of our nerves.

Pupul has not been looking at all well and now she has had to rush off to Bombay because her husband is critically ill.

The grand-children seem to fill the house. Rahul is a darling. Since a few days he has decided to shout rather than speak normally, due either to exuberance or the belief that we are all deaf! It is rather nerve-racking at times and frightening for his little sister.

My thoughts are with you as always.

Love,
Indira

At a 1970 gathering I had arranged for Indira in New York, we discussed Ivan Illich's book Deschooling Society. *Not long after, I went to Mexico, where I met Illich. I told him I thought his book might have great meaning for India, and that I had given a copy to Mrs. Gandhi. Illich's response was that he had no interest in India. Before long he received an invitation from the Indian Education Department to go there; he accepted. Before he departed, I showed him volumes by Ananda K. Coomaraswamy, the*

*renowned Indian art historian, and other instructive In-
dian authors. I was happy to note his new interest in India.*

Prime Minister's House
New Delhi
May 13, 1972

Dorothy dear,
As usual our letters crossed.
Ivan Illich has been invited to come to India and the
invitation has been accepted. I am told that he is an ad-
mirer of Mao. This explains his antipathy to India. However, I do not think we need let this worry us. We want
persons with ideas to stimulate our own people to new
thinking.
A short while ago an interesting seminar on anti-
imperialism was attended by some Left extremists. We
naturally could not convert all. But I think we made some
little dent in the thinking of some of them!

With much love,
Indira

Prime Minster's House
New Delhi
October 4, 1972

Dear Dorothy,
Your letter of September 27, 1972.
Ivan Illich seems to be taking his visit to India seriously. I have heard that he has asked specially to see Jayaprakash Narayan.[1] Vinoba Bhave[2] is a good man, sincere

in his admiration for the Mahatma, but he has always lacked Gandhiji's vision, breadth of understanding and human sympathy. Also, he is surrounded by rather small, narrow-minded people. The Gramdan Movement was a good idea but it has not made much practical impact.

Jayaprakash is a frustrated person and flits from idea to idea. From the very beginning of the Bangladesh crisis he was urging me to march our armies into Bangladesh but by the time the situation actually developed, forcing our action, he was of another view. Right now his theme is that I am the "world's great dictator." This is Morarji Desai's[3] band wagon, now supported by the Jan Sangh[4] on the one hand and the Communist Extremists (Marxist-Leninists) on the other. The Sarvodaya[5] people worked against us in the elections and continue to create confusion.

Meeting you might help I. I. to orient his ideas. I do not know whether he can understand the situation here—so different from Latin America—or that it may be possible, or at least worth the effort, to try and change the establishment from within.

I am genuinely concerned about the present educational system here. I was fortunate to go to institutions and to be with people whose teaching went far beyond the normal routine. But my own experience had made me doubtful about the value of most schools. I am convinced that if we had been able to change our outmoded educational system when we became free it would have made a big difference. We are now trying to see what can be done. Our present Education Minister—who was Head of the History Department of Aligarh University—is a person of understanding. We are inviting I. I. for our own education and in an attempt to clutch at any straw!

I have read Reimer's "Essays on Alternatives in Education" and also Ronald Segal's "The Struggle Against History." I must confess I am attracted by the sort of participatory democracy which they advocate. But how does one bring it about? What I have been trying to do in India is to involve more people in the political processes and to initiate public discussion on education and other important subjects. Public opinion must be formed in favour of changes in the structure of education, of administration, of justice and so on. But will the vested interests allow them to work? We have to contend with human nature. The desire of ninety-nine people out of a hundred is to hang on to whatever power and position they have.

I have just been to a part of the country I had not seen before in spite of my intensive travels—Lahaul and Spiti in the Higher Himalayas. Quite fantastic scenery.

Love,
Indira

1. Narayan had been dedicated to Mahatma Gandhi's nonviolent struggle for India's freedom, before independence. In turn, he was attracted by Marxism, but then rejected it, supported Nehru, and later played the leading role among Indian Socialists. Though a national political figure, he withdrew from organized political life and joined Bhave's Bhoodan movement.
2. A follower of Gandhi and a leader of the Bhoodan or Gramdan movement. Through it, he urged landowners to grant unused acreage to the poor and landless. Many donations were made, but since the areas given were not of the highest quality, no radical changes resulted.
3. Under Nehru, Chief Minister of Bombay; Commerce and Finance Minister. Later, Prime Minister for the Janata Party, which opposed Indira and the Congress Party.
4. A political party whose leaders opposed Congress Party leadership. In general, it was against what it considered excessively leftist or socialist tendencies in Congress. It merged with other opposition parties to form the Janata Party in 1977.
5. Universal good.

Gandhinagar (Ahmedabad)
October 10, 1972

Dorothy dear,

Your letter of the 2nd has reached me here on what must surely be one of the most hectic days I have ever had. Perhaps that is why I am replying immediately!

What you say about the New York [preelection political] function is so familiar. When we got our big majority, I had prophesied that victory brought its own difficulties and dangers. This is what we are now suffering from.

I have not read [Coomaraswamy's] *The Bugbear of Literacy*. I shall see whether I can get hold of it. Neither have I seen the bibliography [about India] prepared by J. Michael Mahar. So cannot comment on it.

I entirely agree with you and our ancient scriptures that the ways to truth are many!

Much love,

Yours in haste,
Indira

Prime Minister's House
New Delhi
October 19, 1972

Dorothy dear,

Naturally Ivan Illich will be free to meet whomever he likes or go wherever he likes.

Our new Education Minister is good and I think it is the Education Ministry which is I. I.'s host. Whatever

I. I.'s allergy to Government, if it is at all intended to use any of his ideas, this can be done only through Government.

Parliament will be sitting November-December. The opposition—all parties, extreme Left and extreme Right included—are said to have finally decided to concentrate on a vilification campaign.

As I wrote earlier, Jayaprakash Narayan is a party to all this.

Much love,
Indira

Raj Bhavan
Shillong, Assam
November 7, 1972

Dorothy dear,

It was lovely to hear from you and to have the photographs of your [East Hampton] Long Island home.

As you see from the address, I am up in Shillong with B. K. and Fory. Rajiv, Sonia, the grandchildren (who are darlings), Sonia's younger sister and Amie Crishna are also here. Up till now I had work but today is a day off more or less. Early tomorrow back to Delhi. Parliament opens on the 13th. A gruesome session it threatens to be!

This is a lovely place. So tranquil and the landscape so gentle. So are the people who are tribals, mostly Khadis. The house used to be dark and dismal but Fory has done wonders for it. She has such lovely things. The garden is quite perfect. Not many flowers but gently undulating irregular lawns, sloping down to a charming little lake which is actually outside the compound but seems to be part of it from here.

I am reading Illich's *The Retooling of Society* and find it absorbing, although I feel he does over-simplify the situation.

I am depressed. The economic situation is extremely difficult but not beyond us. However agitations are brewing or, as reports indicate, being deliberately provoked over such silly non-issues—a quarrel over a cinema ticket in Punjab, the suicide of a Harijan girl in a non-government institution and so on. It is exasperating. In spite of high prices about which there is so much complaining, the two or three festivals—Dudsehra, Diwali—have never been celebrated so spontaneously and extravagantly by the people at large. Huge crowds coming into the towns and cities from the rural areas and buying up practically everything they could lay hands on!

Relationship with the U.S. Yes, that's depressing too. We are told by government people from other countries that since the U.S. is no longer interested in saving Asia from Chinese communism, it is no longer interested in India. That is, India finds no place in its thinking! On the other hand, it would also like to teach us a lesson and hence is pressuring other countries also to withdraw all help. Your elections are over, as expected.[1] What now?

Keep well and look after yourself.

Love,
Indira

1. Richard M. Nixon was reelected President.

Dorothy dear,

Your letter of birthday greetings reached me just on time on the 18th. You will never guess how I spent my birthday. As it was a Sunday, and the next day (today) is also a holiday—Guru Nanak's[1] birthday—I was able to escape the usual crowd (some sincere but many not) who come to greet me, a most exhausting experience—to a place that is only half an hour away from Delhi but is quiet and off the beaten track. The Haryana Government have built some small cottages on a lake called Badkhal, rather bleak and rocky but with a beauty of its own. Amie and I came on the 18th evening and the children spent the 19th with us. It was lovely to have them, although Sanjay's motor boat did shatter the quiet. However I noticed that even this noise did not disturb the water birds or the hippies who seemed to be camping on the far side.

Little Priyanka [Rajiv and Sonia Gandhi's daughter] was not able to come as she is having teething trouble. But Rahul felt very important. First, carrying a huge bouquet of paper flowers to greet me and then steering the motor boat with his hair standing up in the wind!

We had Noam Chomsky[2] for the Nehru Memorial Lecture. As usual they rushed him so much and he had so many speaking engagements that he was utterly exhausted by the time he left. He is [so] unassuming that we all liked him. The Nehru Award for International Understanding went to Mother Teresa.[3] It was a most moving function. She is truly one of God's good people.

With love,
Indira

1. Founder of Sikhism, a religious faith of India.
2. American linguist and author.
3. Roman Catholic nun who works in a Calcutta-based mission that aids needy old people and children. She was awarded the Nobel Peace Prize in 1979.

Prime Minister's House
New Delhi
April 24, 1973

My dear Dorothy,

I have your letter of 13th April and I think a note from you came earlier also.

Pupul is soon going to the States and I am sure you will have the latest news.

This year we in India seem to have more than our share of difficulties. These are partly inherent in the process of growth but aggravated by the war [with Pakistan] and the burden of ten million refugees followed by a terrible drought which has caused shortage of food and drinking water and of power which has affected our industries also. So the Opposition is having a field day.

The Canada trip is more or less firmed up. Yesterday we had [Prime Minister Pierre Elliott] Trudeau's personal representative to discuss the Commonwealth Conference which is being held in August. Since I am going there on a State visit and our Parliament will be in session in August, I do not know if I shall be able to go there again.

Please do not hesitate to write if you feel like [it]. However busy, personal letters especially from someone like you are greatly looked forward to.

The family is well. Rahul is full of talk and noise and the little girl is a perfect doll.

With love,
Indira

Dorothy dear,

Thank you for sending me [William Thompson's] *The Edge of History*—it has opened out quite a new train of thought. Some of his references are beyond me—since it is almost impossible to keep in touch with contemporary Americana.

I have been very moody these days. Except in the early years there has hardly ever been a moment free and available for introspection. To think of the usual questions "who am I and why am I?" Always just ahead was a task to be done which brooked no delay. So it seems strange—on second thought perhaps it is natural and a part of the aging process—to sit and think of myself and of life.

I read somewhere that Karl Marx, when asked about life, said "Life is struggle." Heaven knows I have had struggle enough yet I think of life as wonder. The wonder of nature and the variety of its pulsating life.

The pride and arrogance of youth is long since gone, replaced by a deep humility not only personal but for the whole human race. Aren't we presumptuous in equating ourselves with the world? Does it really matter if the human race as we know it ceases to exist? The earth will continue and probably another species evolve!

I am feeling imprisoned—by the security people who think they can hide their utter incompetence by sheer numbers and a tighter closing in but also and perhaps more so by the realization that I have come to an end, that there's no further growing in this direction. One has friends at school and at various stages of life but comes a time when one outpaces them and leaves them behind.

There can be talk and meeting but no longer the sharing. This is what I feel.

Is it because the situation is so maddeningly frustratingly difficult—because one cannot see a solution—simply because the steps to be taken depend not on a limited group with whom one has rapport and can therefore guide, but on numbers who cannot think beyond their own advantage and find glee in things going wrong. This could be so. But I feel really that the reason is deeper and has been building for some time.

My growth—so intuitive—leaving oneself open to ideas and forces. Our times, for all their complexity or because of it, are truly challenging. It is exasperating to see people enmeshed in pettiness and greed and meanness! They fight for such small things and miss all that is worthwhile.

On the night of the 31st we had a bad air crash. Many friends and acquaintances perished. One of my cabinet ministers also. He came from a wealthy, very conservative Brahmin family of Madras. While in Cambridge he fell for the "idealism" of the Communist party. Except for an intense concern for people and a desire to give, he wasn't a political person. In the early '50's he decided to practice law and did exceedingly well. Soon afterwards he came to the conclusion that my Congress could meet the needs of India. Kamaraj, the chief Minister of Madras, made him the Advocate General of that State. After the last parliamentary elections I took him into the Cabinet to clean up the mess that was our steel production. He did a marvellous job but it was only begun. Quick of mind, eloquent, hard-working—these qualities were combined with total loyalty and dedication. He had a sparkling enthusiasm which was catching.

It is really the early hours of the 4th. The Canadian trip is on but the part I was looking forward to, Fiji and

146

Tonga, has had to be omitted because of the strong feeling that I should not be out for so long.

Love,
Indira

Prime Minister's House
New Delhi
June 11, 1974

Dorothy dear,

Just a line to send you my love.

As you say the whole world is "in a mess" yet when one looks closely, many long-standing problems are being solved. Perhaps that is life itself—a mixture of good and bad. But because of the advance of science and technology, everything is so much faster and on such a vaster scale and hence more complex.

I believe the press has made a big fuss of my alleged fall from a horse. I did not fall but I did manage to fracture the third finger of my left hand as I was dismounting from a horse.

Love,
Indira

At the time of the Chinese invasion of India, in 1962, and again in 1971, during India's war with Pakistan, a state of emergency was declared in India. Equally plaguing situations arose after these periods. By 1974, rioting and antigovernment demonstrations became widespread. In Bihar State, youth and student groups protested against the government and the police. Many from other states joined the movement by objecting bitterly to existing conditions throughout the country. There was some fear that the army might further disrupt the situation. General disorder and unease gained ground. Moreover, Prime Minister Gandhi was faced by a court case that had originated in 1971 which accused her of election malpractices.

On June 25, 1975, she declared an unprecedented state of internal emergency. The nature of her act shocked defenders of democracy and startled proponents of civil rights. Friends of India and many Indians who had long worked to help in the struggle for freedom could not at first believe the news.

Those of us in New York who had been staunch advocates of a free India asked ourselves whether conditions there were, in fact, so distressing that abrogation of civil liberties had to be as extreme as the press reported. Was it necessary to postpone, then cancel, general elections? Why were leading critics of the government arrested and imprisoned without specific charges being made against them and without their having the right of habeas corpus? Why was the press under strict government control?

After waiting for what we considered a reasonable time, we realized, with a pang, that the alarming actions were correctly reported. I called a meeting of those perturbed by the emergency measures. We issued a statement that expressed our concern. Sidney Hertzberg, former U.S. correspondent for the Hindustan Times *of New Delhi, Indian-born author Ved Mehta, and I drafted a joint appeal, which read, in part:*

"We are Americans concerned with maintaining and furthering human rights, and our concern extends to all people throughout the world. Consequently, we are distressed by the loss of fundamental human rights in India following the proclamation of a national emergency there on June 25, 1975.

*"We deplore these events, especially in India, because
there democracy was established after a long struggle for
freedom led by some of the greatest contemporary expo-
nents of human rights, and also because the respect of
democratic India for these human rights was for so many
years a beacon light for all newly independent and developing countries.*

*"Experience shows that when human rights are sup-
pressed anywhere they are threatened everywhere, and that
the longer they are suppressed the longer it takes to restore
them. We therefore call for the restoration of these rights
in India."*

*We sent our appeal to widely known and respected in-
dividuals, eighty of whom signed it. We released it to the
press, radio, and television, and tried to publicize it in India as best we could. We learned that it reached and heart-
ened the underground there, and that the government was
not pleased. I also held several meetings for Indian dissi-
dents.*

*After the emergency, I wrote to Indira, expressing my
perplexity. I asked Indians returning to New Delhi to
mention my confusion, and I sent a further note to Indira
about my fear that censorship would draw a curtain of
darkness over India's youth. Not only was internal censorship a danger, but so was the prohibition against allowing
any foreign printed material to enter India. I received three
short notes from her.*

Prime Minister's House
New Delhi
September 19, 1975

Dorothy dear,

If you can bear to accept a gift from the "Great Dictator," here is something which I had kept for you some years ago—it is from Bhutan.

I have been wanting to write to you since June but it is always fatal to wait for a "more leisurely moment" in which to do so.

While I write, the Chief Minister of Kerala is watching me patiently. So,

Love,
Indira

Prime Minister's House
New Delhi
June 30, 1976

Dear Dorothy,

Your letter of the 20th has just reached me.

I am up to the eyes in sorting out papers and other matters before I leave for East Germany and Afghanistan tomorrow. A few hours after my return, I shall get involved with the Conference of Information Ministers of the Non-aligned countries, in preparation for the Summit Meeting in August in Colombo.

I have thought of you a great deal and long wanted to write. If I can get a moment either on the plane or on my return, I shall write in detail.

Pupul is planning to go to the States some time soon. But even she is not fully in the know of the situation as it had developed here, or of the matters which we are now discovering.

With love,
Indira

New Delhi
December 25, 1976

Dorothy dear,

Thank you for your messages. There is so much I wanted to write to you about and I had put this card aside for the purpose. But Christmas is already here so I hasten to send my love and good wishes.

Indira

Indira Gandhi called for elections in 1977, and was decisively voted out of power. The Janata Party, a merger of five smaller political parties, in opposition to Mrs. Gandhi and the Congress Party, unseated her. Despite its complaints and its own promises, it failed to do a satisfactory job. It was defeated in 1980. Indira became Prime Minister once more.

(Since Indira and I did not correspond during the emergency period, facts about it, and about the activities of her younger son, Sanjay Gandhi, lie outside the scope of this volume.)

I sent a note to Indira in 1980 after Sanjay was killed in an airplane crash. I wrote to her as woman to woman about her loss.

My letter:

East Hampton, N.Y.
June 24, 1980

Indira,

My heart aches for you in your overwhelming tragedy. I feel very close to you and wish I could be with you. I hope you

151

will never forget conversations we had some years ago when you were going through a difficult period. I told you then that if ever you were in need of help, you could count on me. Times have changed, but my hand is still extended to you. At that time I felt a sister to you. Profound feelings do not change, although other things may.

This brings you a special sense of sympathy and of friendship.

Dorothy

———————

Prime Minister's House
New Delhi
August 3, 1980

Dear Dorothy,

It was good of you to write. I have been thinking of writing to you. But it was difficult to know where to begin and I cannot go into all those controversies now.

Seldom has any person had to brave such hardship and such a sustained campaign of calumny. It is to Sanjay's credit that he retained his dignity and calmness of spirit and to the end was a help and a joy to have around the house.

I have not changed. It is sad that people do not care to look beyond the newspaper reports or the slanderous remarks of individuals who have always opposed us. As Pupul will have told you, my friendships are constant.

I was especially glad to hear from you.

Yours sincerely,
Indira

My letter:

East Hampton, N.Y.
August 6, 1980

Indu dear,

It is so long since we have corresponded, at one level I do not quite know to whom I am writing; at another level, I am writing to the person I did know. You have been through so much. I am sure that much of the tragedy has transformed you in many ways. I know the great task you have now and how difficult it must be, as well as the tragic events you have suffered.

I have been reading our early correspondence. How lovely it is and how clearly it reveals the delicate person I knew. From the moment we met there seemed to be a true harmony.

How I wish I could see you. How I wish we could talk—although silence, perhaps, would be as revealing as any words. For the moment, I send this letter as a bridge. Friendships are more precious than ever in this so often harsh world.

Love,
Dorothy

Prime Minister's House
New Delhi
September 14, 1980

Dorothy dear,

I have begun several letters to you, but for lack of time and the difficulty in finding the right words, have got no further. When one has much to say, one does not know where to begin.

Your letters have touched me deeply, for you know

153

how fond I have been and have remained of you. And that is why the last years I have felt sad. I do not want to enter into controversy. The past is over, let it lie. But some things have to be said. The falsehood, the persistent malicious campaign of calumny must be refuted.

You know me well enough to appreciate that I am neither authoritarian nor cold. But I am not effusive, and perhaps this is misunderstood.

We now face a terribly difficult situation economically and politically. The opposition parties which spoke up so loudly for democracy did not accept the people's verdict in our 1971–72 elections and they have not accepted it in 1980. There is utter indiscipline and many agitations all over the place. Can a developing country develop in these circumstances? Can the poor or the underprivileged have a chance of making their voice heard or of exerting their rights?

This has become much longer than I intended and also something like a lecture! But I am sure you will understand that I write out of friendship.

I hope you are feeling better. Pupul is here in Delhi for some days, trying to help on the cultural side which like much else is in a thorough mess.

Much love,
Indira

Prime Minister's House
New Delhi
February 21, 1981

Dear Dorothy,

I do believe in myself. Perhaps that is what has brought so much trouble. I also seem to have an aptitude to take on the worries and troubles of others. Long ago in my early childhood my grandfather used to joke that if there was a more difficult path, I could be trusted to find it. This was on our summer trips to the mountains. I loved them then as I do now. Instead of going on the regular road, I preferred to climb straight up the steep side in spite of loose earth and rocks and roots which cropped up unexpectedly all over the place.

Sanjay's going has affected me profoundly. As a Bulgarian girl said this morning "You do not weep outside but deep within." Yet isn't this very selfish? Basically we do not weep for those who have gone but for ourselves. Also there are certain events which are difficult to narrate in a letter.

It is good to have Pupul in Delhi. She lives closeby. Yet we have not yet been to her house. She often drops in to a meal. She is full of ideas and there is so much to do but the bureaucracy is not only exasperating in its bureaucratic methods and delays but it seems is deliberately hampering our work.

Love,
Indira

Baur au Lac
Zurich
May 9, 1981

Dorothy dear,

Pupul phoned from New York and I sent my good wishes. I was glad to hear that you are feeling better.

This brief visit to Switzerland seems a rather unusual interlude after the more than hectic routine of the last many years. Even so there were many visitors, some of whom had come from other countries. But between the W.H.O. [World Health Organization] programme in Geneva, a fleeting visit to my old school in the hills (also the lovely graceful old chalets now modernised), lunch with the Swiss president and the final lap in Zurich I managed an evening and part of the next morning at a heavenly lakeside Chateau Hotel. It will be a memory like Wordsworth's host of daffodils!

I'm well—or at least as well as one can be in this crazy, upside down world. I think of you and send my love.

Indira

In the autumn of 1981, Indira Gandhi went to Canada to a Commonwealth conference, then to Cancun, Mexico, for another international meeting. There were messages about the possibility of my joining her, either in Canada or at Lake Placid, where she hoped to meet two old friends. She and I did not manage to get together. Her time became too limited, and I could not work out a plan whereby I could quickly obtain adequate transport.

Cancun, Mexico

October 23, 1981

Dorothy dear,

What a pleasure to hear your voice even on the phone. I would so have loved the opportunity of meeting you but it really wasn't possible. The short time we had in Montreal was full of official calls and other business. By the time I was free it was late and I was dead beat. I tried to phone you from my room but without success. The same thing has happened today. I am told there is no relief.

Cancun was an interesting experience and an opportunity of meeting people. Old friends and new faces. I can't say that much has come out of it except that we each had our say. Tomorrow we leave.

This is just a rushed message to send my love and wish you well.

Indira

A large-scale Indian Arts Festival—"Aditi"—was held in London in 1982. It had the full and enthusiastic backing of the Indian and British governments. It created a sensation. Indian villagers came and practiced their traditional crafts with extraordinary dexterity. India's classical art was also exhibited.

Pupul Jayakar was the Indian Chairman of the Festival. She and Indira came to London for the opening; Indira had Pupul phone, inviting me to join them, even though the program had not yet been fully worked out. Because of ill-health, I could not travel at the time.

Prime Minister's House
New Delhi
December 23, 1981

Dorothy dear,

I have two letters from you regarding London. I did not reply as I was awaiting some indication of the programme in London, which would enable me to say something definite. This has not yet come. But a friend who is on the Festival Committee passed through Delhi and has given us a vague outline—it is difficult to judge its authenticity. According to this, the schedule is extremely crowded and some of the items still have to be fitted in.

Needless to say, I should be delighted to meet you, after all these years. We must try to find a way. Unfortunately, this is the time of our budget session of Parliament when absence from Delhi is not advisable or possible to prolong.

Anyhow I am figuring out how to manage and shall let you know as soon as we ourselves have a clear idea of the schedule.

Pupul and I often talk of you—but these days I am so terribly overworked, we haven't been able to meet. These are the last days of what we call the winter session of Parliament, hence the greater pressure for appointments with M.P.s and meetings of all kinds.

Tomorrow is Christmas eve. The grandchildren are busy decorating the tree which arrived only this afternoon from Simla.

Excuse this piece of scribble. I am in the midst of a meeting.

My love to you and all good wishes. Be well.

Indira

Prime Minister's House
New Delhi
January 22, 1982

Dorothy dear,

Pupul has been trying to get in touch with you on my behalf for days and days, but in vain. No one lifted the phone. Perhaps you are away from New York.

The day before yesterday a rather attractive woman (I did not quite catch her title), Elizabeth de Cuevas,[1] came to see me. She claimed to be a friend of yours and to have met you just before coming to India. She said something about your being in East Hampton. Pupul, on the other hand, says it is much too cold there in winter, especially this particular winter which is exceptional in North Europe and America.

The reason for trying to contact you is my unhappiness at what seems to be a misunderstanding created by my last letter to you. I did not say I was too busy to meet you. On the contrary, Pupul and I are determined to keep some meals free as well as time for talks. The dates of the visit are definite but we do not yet have the formal programme from the British or from our own High Commission, so it is difficult to fix timings right now.

I do hope you can come to London if you are well enough. I am looking forward to meeting you.

With love,
Indira

1. American sculptor.

Prime Minister's House
New Delhi
June 13, 1982

Dorothy dear,

A couple of days ago I had an undated letter from you. It is obviously written before our Ambassador spoke to you again. It is good to see your hand-writing again.

I am looking forward to meeting you and do hope you can come down to New York. I have told the Ambassador that I shall keep Saturday evening and Sunday free. But I do want to go to the theatre, if it is possible. Naturally it would be lovely to have you along and I hope that it is not too tiring for you.

Pupul suggests that I should see *Amadeus*. We had taken tickets for it in London when I was there for just an evening on the way back from Cancun. The I.R.A. threw a couple of bombs in that area, so the British security would not allow me to go. Have you any other suggestion? Also, are theatres open on Sunday (they are not in London)? I should like at least one theatre evening kept free.

Pupul feels I should also see the new Greek collection at the Metropolitan Museum and as I am lunching there on the 28th, I may fit it in then. Pupul's other suggestion is to see the Rockefeller Collection of Primitive Art and to go to Bonwit Teller, her favourite shop. Also, a bookshop.

I do hope you are well. I'm looking forward to meeting you.

With love,
Indira

Indira Gandhi came to New York briefly in the summer of 1982, accompanied by her son Rajiv and Sonia. She invited me to lunch and then to see Peter Shaffer's Amadeus. *Our meeting would be the first in many years.*

Because I had made clear and public my position against the 1975 emergency, I assumed that our relationship might not be as warm as it had been in the past. Indira must also have realized that I, like many other critics of the emergency, had been upset that such widespread corruption still existed in India. She herself had often complained to me about it. I had no way of judging why she had been unable to curb it. I knew that much had gone wrong, even though I realized also the difficulties she faced. I could not imagine what we would feel when we met.

Here before me would stand a woman who had long headed a highly complex society of some seven hundred million people, most of them poor and faced with manifold problems; a woman recently overwhelmed by grief over her son's death.

She had once written to me questioning whether we did not all, at different times, have different personalities. I had not known the Indira of the emergency. Had she, as some claimed, ceased dominating political life in India, and allowed it to control her? I would never know.

Was I forever to hold against her what had happened in the seventies? She was not, after all, a fascist or a Nazi; she had said there would be no further emergencies, and there had been none. Clearly she was reaching out to me for continued friendship, not for forgiveness.

As I entered Indira's suite at the Carlyle Hotel, I had no time to formulate my position. The instantly warm nature of our reunion dictated our actions. Our meeting was as spontaneously sympathetic as any we had had before. We were glad to see one another again.

I found no visible change in Indira as a person. Her face was sad, but not entirely. There were sudden shafts of radiance as we spoke. Obviously, our views of what had happened would never be identical. But each was clearly experiencing the stability of a firmly based friendship. What might well have set us apart had not done so. As we spoke I had a warm feeling, too, about Rajiv and Sonia. I had known Rajiv as a child in 1950, then as a young man, when he stayed at our home with Indira, and now I saw him as a fine adult.

The Carlyle
New York, N.Y.
August 2, 1982

Dear dear Dorothy,

How lovely it was to have some time with you—not enough. There is so much to say, which one can only get across to someone who understands and can see things from a distance. It is frustrating to begin and not be able to go on.

Yes, I am quieter, sadder. Yet is it hardly fair to want more? Life has given of its fullness to me, in happiness and in pain. How can one know one without the other?

I do want to write, but for that I must be freer. I have always been close to the earth and the net of protocol and security is particularly galling.

Is it because of age that one thinks things everywhere are deteriorating? And this at a time when there is so much more excellence and even creativity in people. [W. B.] Yeats said things fall apart, the centre does not hold. What is the centre, and where?

There is much to question and to share. But this is just to send my love.

Indira

Prime Minister's House
New Delhi
August 22, 1982

Dorothy dear,

I wrote a few lines to you from Honolulu or Tokyo. I hope you got the letter.

It was indeed a joy to meet you. I wish we could have had a longer period for just talking.

After a certain age the past often looks rosier, so I do not know if it is age, but I do feel that the world is becoming a nastier place to live in. The glare of publicity focuses not on what is actually happening but tries to search out something wrong or sensational.

In India the spreading of false rumours is almost an industry. I shall give two examples, one old and one new—Miss Naidu, not Padmaja, but her younger sister Lilamani (who was totally different: very very thin, with a brilliant mind and a heart of gold), introduced me to two American women, Mrs. Kyle and Miss Carson in the early 50s. Since then they come to India every other year and always visit me. There was no intimate friendship but just a pleasant fellow-feeling in view of their affection and concern for India. When I went to Canada in 1981, Mrs. Kyle was very ill and wanted very much that I should go to meet her. They used to live partly in Montreal and partly at Lake Placid. I thought I would motor across but the Canadian Government very kindly lent a small plane. Amie Crishna and I flew to Lake Placid, were with them for barely fifteen minutes to say hello, met some of their friends and rushed back to Montreal. Afterwards I was told that enquiries had been made whether I had come for any financial transactions! Something identical has occurred now.

A certain couple were introduced to my father and me way back in 1942 by Mrs. Sarojini Naidu.[1] They married a month and a half before I did and lived in our neighbourhood in Allahabad. We both had two sons of more or less the same ages, who grew up together in Delhi. Some years ago their elder son became one of our more glamorous film stars (though I cannot say that I enjoy the violence of his films). On the eve of our departure for the United States he had an accident. In Los Angeles, a message came that his condition was critical. Had I been in India our whole family would have gone to Bombay to be with them all. As it was, we decided that Rajiv should fly back and on my return to Delhi, Sonia and I also went down to Bombay for a few hours. When one is battling for one's life or indeed for anything else, it makes an enormous difference if close friends are there to help build morale. Again, the story was spread that the purpose of our visits was because of financial deals. And all this when we don't even have the means to finish the building of our small house! The whole atmosphere is so sordid and there seems to be no value attached to friendship and other human emotions.

I am off to Mauritius and Mozambique very early to-morrow.

This was not meant to burden you with a long story but just to send my love.

Indira

P.S. Pupul just came and another even worse slander was discussed.

1. Great Indian poet and devoted follower of Mahatma Gandhi.

Prime Minister's House
New Delhi
September 1, 1982

Dear Dorothy,

Just a hurried line to thank you for your lovely letter and the note which came with the books. I look forward to reading the two novels. I have Bucky Fuller's book. But isn't he difficult to read? I can only manage short bits at a time. He is an old friend who has been visiting here fairly regularly on his way to and from Japan or somewhere. He cabled for an appointment before I left for New York and I, in turn, asked our Ambassador to fix time for him. But on arrival I was told that nobody knew where he was and also that probably he was not well.

Love,
Indira

P.S. On my return from a one day visit to the U.P. [United Provinces] I found more books, all new to me. Thank you again.

Various Indian friends had been urging me to visit India, but it was not possible for me to travel.

Prime Minister's House
New Delhi
September 14, 1982

Dorothy dear,

Your letters of the 25th and 26th August came together yesterday. They have been travelling up and down to office with me these two days. But I have only just had the time to read them. I can hardly find the words to say how touched I feel, and I do understand.

It would give me enormous pleasure to have you here in India. I do not yet know my programme. I shall let you know as soon as I can. I am not involved in ASIAD [Asian Games] except for the opening ceremony. But the winter

is busier than other times because of a stream of high dignitaries and others coming from various parts of the world
as well as our own Republic Day celebrations in January,
and various other commitments. However, this does not
mean that I wouldn't have time to meet you and talk with
you which, let me assure you, I enjoy doing.

All the time I was there, London was sunny, very
pleasant and not at all cold. I think I wore a jersey when
I went out but did not need a coat.

I shall probably be in Delhi most of November. Of
course there will be Parliament until the 5th but that
doesn't matter, time can be found.

With love,
Indira

Prime Minister's House
New Delhi
November 10, 1982

Dorothy dear,

I do not know if I have replied to your latest letter.
You have been much in my mind and I have been writing
to you mentally, but just did not have time to put my
thoughts on paper. I was looking forward to your coming
to Delhi and am sorry that this was not possible. However it is a relief that you had to give up the trip because
of your book and not because of ill health. Do look after
yourself even if it sometimes seems rather a bore.

The winter months are always extremely busy and this
year our problems are compounded by agitations which
in spite of protestations do and have turned violent. I
usually go out of my way to be conciliatory and to consider any demand which is reasonable. However, some

have wide financial implications which we cannot afford and others might weaken the country's unity or affect different States so that a piecemeal solution would create widespread problems in many States. Besides all this, we have the Asian Games in a few days. Some Opposition Parties have been against them from the very beginning. It is a peculiar attitude. When the Janata Party Government was in power, some of its members decided to oppose a purely private venture—an International Motor Car Rally—and went as far as to stone it, smashing the French participant's car. Mr. Mitterrand and perhaps Mr. Mubarak of Egypt are also coming this month.[1]

In spite of all this I had managed to keep time every evening for our talks. Now I shall see if I can evoke the same response on paper in my letters to you.

J. Krishnamurti was here. He has a certain quality and in spite of his pessimism, radiates serenity.

Pupul has gone off to London for the winding up of the [Indian Arts] Festival.

With love,
Indira

1. François Mitterrand, President of France, and Hosni Mubarak, President of Egypt.

Prime Minister's House
New Delhi
December 2, 1982

Dear Dorothy,

Your letter of the 20th November. I love to hear from you. Our friendship has a lightness yet a permanent quality.

How strange is life. What is real and what of our imagination or making? Our view of people and of history is conditioned by historians, biographers, commentators. But when one sees how present day events are presented and even distorted, how true is the picture we have of any person or happening?

The Gandhi film[1] has opened with much fanfare. It is impressive. It is good for the world to know what Gandhiji stood for. Yet for those who lived through those times, the film is a spectacle, grand and powerful, yet lacking some essential quality—the spirit that is India. The tragedy is that no Indian film maker has been inspired by the greatness and the drama of that magnificent mass movement or the remarkable men and women (almost every district has its heroes and heroines) who led it. Gandhiji was the crest of the wave. The film makes him a dramatic "super star" type of messiah—not more than he was but rather less by diminishing the other factors.

Rajiv has done a magnificent job with our Asiad (as the Asian games are called). Many have cooperated, working hard and with dedication but watching it all, I have no doubt that it is Rajiv's own effort, his organizing capacity, aim at excellence, and concern for the minutest detail that enabled us not only to be ready on time, but, as we are told by the Heads of the various international Sports Associations who have come, to attain international standards in our constructions and all other arrangements. The opening ceremony was spectacular.

Our newspapers are, as usual, trying desperately hard to look under the carpet for a grain of dirt or a flaw, so the concentration is on the amount spent. How does one measure the enthusiasm and hope of young people? The games have been more educational than any institution. They have drawn together the city and the village and given a new perspective to our young people. No newspaper comments on the expenses in terms of money, goods and even lives of all the futile agitations that take place all the time.

Mitterrand was here. He is different from most other Heads whom I have met and especially your own President. Have you read his *Wheat and the Chaff*? He loves literature and nature and seems to make a genuine effort to understand. He is a good friend of Márquez[2] who has invited him to the Nobel Prize ceremony. Mrs. Mitterrand will go. The day that Mitterrand left, Mubarak of Egypt arrived. So life goes on.

You are often in my thoughts.

Love,
Indira

1. *Gandhi*, produced and directed by Richard Attenborough, starring Ben Kingsley.
2. Gabriel García Márquez, Colombian author and winner of the Nobel Prize for Literature.

———————————

In flight
New Delhi–Assam
February 10, 1983

Dorothy dear,

Thank you for your letters. I was putting off replying until I had more time but you must be wondering if the letters are reaching me.

What has moved me to write now is the truly magnificent view of the snow covered Himalayan Range. We are close enough to identify many of the most famous peaks which are the world's highest mountains. This is a sight which never fails to thrill me. It is like Wordsworth's daffodils, an ever refreshing memory picture.

I am on a flight to Assam. It is not going to be a pleasant trip. Our Constitution compels us to hold elections every five years. We can postpone them by constitutional amendment. But when this idea was put to the Opposition parties they did not agree to support us and our strength in the Upper House is not sufficient to act by ourselves. Now that the elections have been announced and the process is taking its inevitable course, some of the Opposition parties are pressing for postponement. Apart from the constitutional aspect, nobody seems to be concerned about the terrible violence, murders, sabotage and so on of the agitators who are terrorising the rest of the population, kidnapping candidates, attacking officials and so on. They have killed nearly 190 people in the last four years. This does not include 1983 or the election period. However serious the grievance or just any demand, how can any country be held together if such pressures are brought to bear on the Government. Had the Opposition parties not encouraged the agitation, I am sure a solution would have been found by now, as at several meetings we were on the brink of an agreement, which the students refuted within a few hours of their return to Assam!

Pupul was to go off to Paris today just for three days or so.

Love,
Indira

Indira planned to come to New York in 1983 for United Nations meetings.

In flight
Madras-Ahmedabad
May 26, 1983

Dear Dorothy,

It is always good to hear from you. Before your letter of May 16 reached me, Pupul was back from the States and gave me news of you. I am sorry that you are not feeling any better, and have difficulty in moving about.

The dates of my visit to New York are the 26th September to 1st October. Needless to say I should love to have some time with you. At this moment the programme is not fixed—it will be full of meetings. If it is at all possible—but I am not promising anything—I should like to take a day off and come up to East Hampton. If I cannot come to East Hampton, I hope we shall find time, as I did on my last visit for a long talk. But will you be well enough to come to New York, if it is not too inconvenient?

Just as I was leaving on this tour, Pupul told me that she would like to be in the United States when I am there, as she wants to pursue certain matters connected with our exhibition[1] there.

With love,
Indira

1. The Indian Arts Festival of 1985.

Prime Minister's House
New Delhi
August 18, 1983

Dorothy dear,

I have been very remiss in replying to your letters.

171

This does not mean any lack of appreciation for or pleasure in receiving them but merely that the days are getting increasingly hectic and crowded with one crisis piling over another.

I have your latest letter of August 3rd. I have about five days in New York and I am trying desperately to make time for something besides the official schedule.

I think of you often and Pupul and I talk about you.

With love,
Indira

Prime Minister's House
New Delhi
August 23, 1983

Dorothy dear,

I don't think I have replied to some of your letters and I seem to have mislaid the latest one in which you have written about my book "Eternal India." I did not bring it for you as it is rather superficial. Actually it isn't my book. The French photographer Nou had interviewed me during my previous regime. One day he turned up at 12-Willingdon Crescent and asked that now that I had more time, could I write a few lines of introduction to his book of photographs of India? Without knowing what it was about I accepted! (My father and Stella Kramrisch[1] have dealt with this subject so much more exhaustively.)

Then I got involved in the State Assembly elections in the South. Suddenly came an SOS that the publication of the book was held up. I took just about four or five days off and took Pupul with me to Coorg to help. I had only a vague idea of the photographs to be used. I have no rights on the book.

Another book has appeared in my name with the ridiculous title "My Truth." This is based on two long interviews with Mr. Pouchpadas. He has added extracts from my writings, speeches and other interviews. So far as I know the words are mine but the book is actually brought out by him. I shall bring you both the books. Mr. Pouchpadas now lives in France.

As time goes on, my programme in New York becomes more and more full. But I hope that somehow I can make an evening free.

Love,
Indira

1. Distinguished authority on Indian art and tradition.

We did get together during her visit. Although she attended numerous meetings, we had a quiet dinner together at her hotel and were relieved that we could talk in private. I sensed that our friendship was more firmly based and relaxed than ever.

The evening of September 30, we heard Puccini's La Bohème. *Neither of us had seen it since we were young, and we had not cherished it at that phase of our lives. Now, as a result of an invitation Indira had received, we were seated in the center parterre box at the Metropolitan Opera House.*

Subdued as always in public, Indira looked fit, alert, elegant. The functions she had attended during the day had not seemed to weary her.

In one scene, Indira's and my eyes met. We looked into one another, then instantly turned away. It was as though we not only understood ourselves and one another, but were witnessing a universal situation. A magic moment.

Afterward, in her limousine, exhilarated, she quoted poetry.

At the opera I mentioned that the film star Luise Rainer, who lived abroad, was in New York. I had introduced her to Indira in London in 1962. Indira and I were to lunch together the next day; she suggested that I ask Luise to join us. She admired Luise's beauty and her vivid personality.

Throughout the 1983 visit, I was concerned about Indira's security; I also was full of wonder about how beautiful our relationship had been since we first met, and how, despite all vicissitudes, it had blossomed.

What had brought us together so immediately in 1949? We had shared our sense of heartbreak and delight throughout the years. We never theorized, but always were open in spirit. The enigmas of the inner world are quite as awe-inspiring as those of the outer universe.

I heard from Indira after her departure, but my own last notes to her in 1984 said only, "Protect yourself. Protect yourself."

In flight
Visakhapatnam–New Delhi
October 11, 1983

Dear Dorothy,

Just a line to say what a joy it was to meet you again. You were looking thin and rather tired. But I hope that cooler weather will now help you to recoup.

It was so good of you to bring Luise Rainer to lunch. What a beautiful and expressive face she still has. She praised the *La Traviata*[1] film. But the review in New York is not good.

I came back very tired as I was getting up much too early all the days I was in New York. Fortunately the hotel, although rather gaudy in its entrance, was comfortable and we were well looked after, and this made the difference. Since coming back, I have been listening to the cassettes you gave me. Feroze was very keen on Beethoven and all these years since his death, I had put away my records. It was a delight to hear the Ninth Symphony again.

As usual I am dictating this on a flight. Because of the Korean tragedy in Rangoon,[2] the Korean president, who was due in Delhi today, cancelled his entire Eastern tour. This gave me time to rush down to the South to make an aerial survey of floods which have caused a great deal of damage especially to the paddy crops and to the huts of the poorest people.

I wish I could have a couple of quiet days in New York. Perhaps it is because I have been so far removed from such leisure and quiet in my life, that I have got such quietness within myself. As I am dictating, a line from an old Indian film comes to mind, "What has he to do with flowers, whose fate is shaped amongst thorns"! But there is hardly a flower without thorns.

With affectionate greetings,
Indira

1. Franco Zeffirelli's film version of the Verdi opera.
2. On October 9, seventeen members of a visiting South Korean delegation, including four ministers, were killed in a terrorist bomb blast.

Prime Minister's House
New Delhi
April 5, 1984

My dear Dorothy,

I don't like sending you typed letters but I want to spare your eyes with my handwriting. Also, there seems to be less and less time. Your letters reach me from time to time. Needless to say they bring me joy. Now Pupul must have met you and given you all the news.

The situation here is a disturbing one. I wish America would be more understanding and interested in the stability and progress of our whole sub-continent. I do believe that this would be of benefit to both our countries.

With love,
Indira

In flight
Silchar-Delhi
April 17, 1984

Dorothy dear,

I have a number of letters from you, each of which I cherish because it brings your loving thoughts.

Pupul is lucky to have met you. She must have told you of the terrible period we are going through here. I am truly depressed.

I hope you are feeling better.

Love,
Indira

My last letter from Indira Gandhi:

Prime Minister's House
New Delhi
May 4, 1984

Dorothy dear,

Pupul is back and gave me the records and your letter last night. These days I have been rather depressed, so they were all the more welcome.

Thinking of you and with love. Be well.

Indira

To the end, while attending to her tasks as Prime Minister, Indira Gandhi reached out to beauty, to nature. Flowers, color, loveliness—like Wordsworth's "host of daffodils"—still nourished her.

Her husband, Feroze Gandhi, had been the first to make her aware of classical Western music. She developed a most sensitive ear for it. In New York, she asked me to send her Bach cassettes, so she could listen to their soothing harmonies while she worked. Shortly before her death, after a day of strenuous activity, she watched Jane Eyre *on television with Rajiv's and Sonia's daughter.*

It seems somehow ironically right that, in the morning, October 31, 1984, in addition to carrying out her manifold responsibilities, she was on the way to be interviewed by that accomplished theater personality Peter Ustinov. All artists—in any medium—were revivifying for her.

Although she knew she might be murdered, she went on with her life as she always had, fearless to the last. She said, "I would rather die standing up, than lying down." She did not reach Mr. Ustinov. Instead, ghastly headlines screamed to the world that Prime Minister Indira Gandhi had been assassinated. Over twenty bullets entered her body. She had, to avoid discrimination, retained certain Sikh guards, whose job was to protect her; they were involved in causing her death.

Pupul Jayakar, our mutually close friend, mentioned often in Indira's letters, wrote to me after the tragedy:
"The horror of the whole thing. She had such élan, such grace, such lightness of foot. She had a fluid mind, could look with clear eyes into the situation around her, could find time for the significant things of life even though the pressures of the immediate were so complex.
"Three days earlier I had met her. She was going the next day to Srinagar [Kashmir]. She said she wanted to go as she had never seen the Chinar leaves turn brilliant red and orange in Autumn. She spoke of one of the oldest Chinar trees in the Valley; she had just heard that it died.
"The last time I saw her, she spoke at length of death. I am glad that her face was untouched by the assassins' bullets. She looked extremely beautiful and at peace."

A further note from Pupul, from New Delhi:
"Amongst Indira's papers, the beginnings of a Will have been discovered. She had premonitions of her violent death."
From the Will:

[Undated]

"I have never felt less like dying and that calm and peace of mind is what prompts me to write what is in the nature of a will.

"If I die a violent death as some fear and a few are

plotting, I know the violence will be in the thought and the action of the assassin, not in my dying—for no hate is dark enough to overshadow the extent of my love for my people and my country; no force is strong enough to divert me from my purpose and my endeavour to take this country forward.

"A poet has written of his 'love'—'how can I feel humble with the wealth of you beside me!' I can say the same of India. I cannot understand how anyone can be an Indian and not be proud—the richness and infinite variety of our composite heritage, the magnificence of the people's spirit, equal to any disaster or burden, firm in their faith, gay spontaneously even in poverty and hardship."

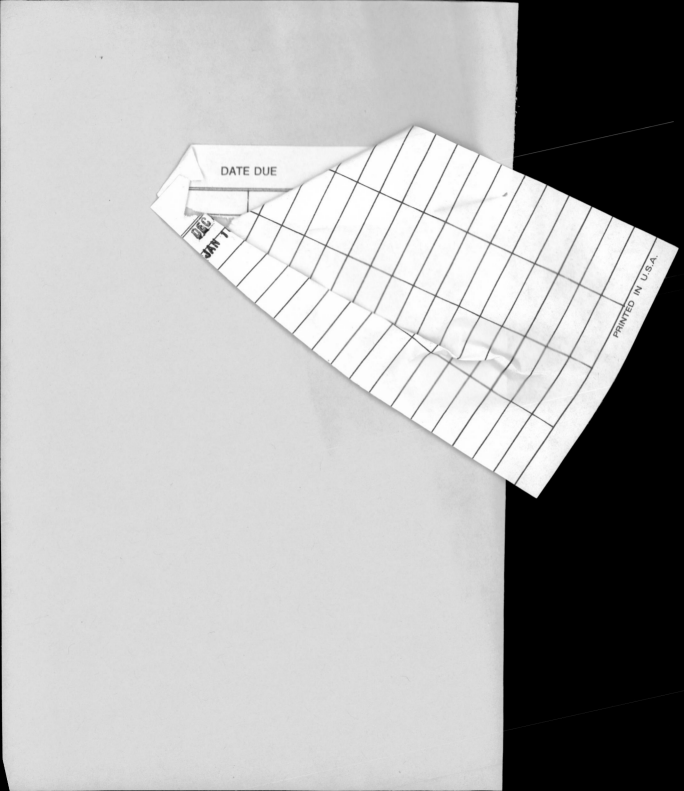

DATE DUE

DEC

JAN 1

PRINTED IN U.S.A.